JOURNEY *to the* SEVENTH CONTINENT

A PHOTO EXPEDITION

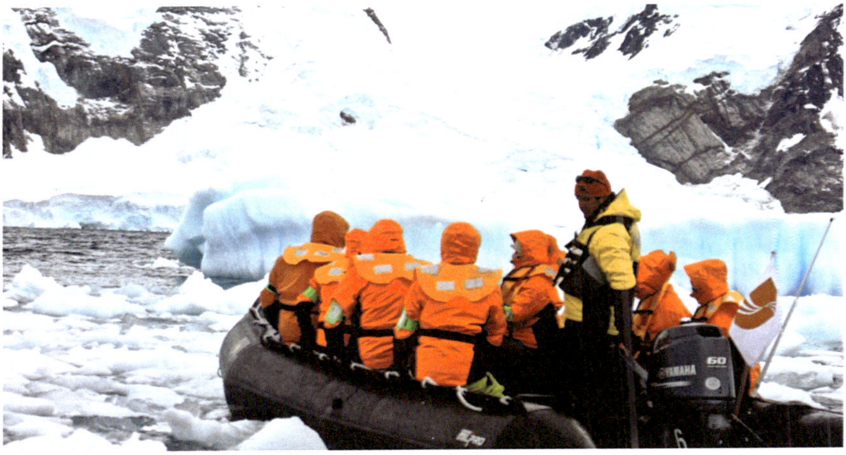

978-1-7398104-9-8 (Paperback)
978-1-7398544-1-6 (e-book)
978-1-7398544-0-9 (Hard Cover)

Printed in the United Kingdom

AEGA Design Publishing Ltd
Kemp House, 160 City Road, London
EC1V 2NX United Kingdom
www.aegadesign.co.uk
info@aegadesign.co.uk

AEGA PUBLISHING

I know the “authors of this book”. It’s very interesting if you’re into seeing places you may otherwise not see. I keep it sitting out so guests can look through it and always feel like I would rather have some of the photos on my wall rather than tucked away in a book.

– WADE BOZEMAN

Amazing photos and an inspiration for people of any age to have such experiences.

– PC

WHAT A JOURNEY

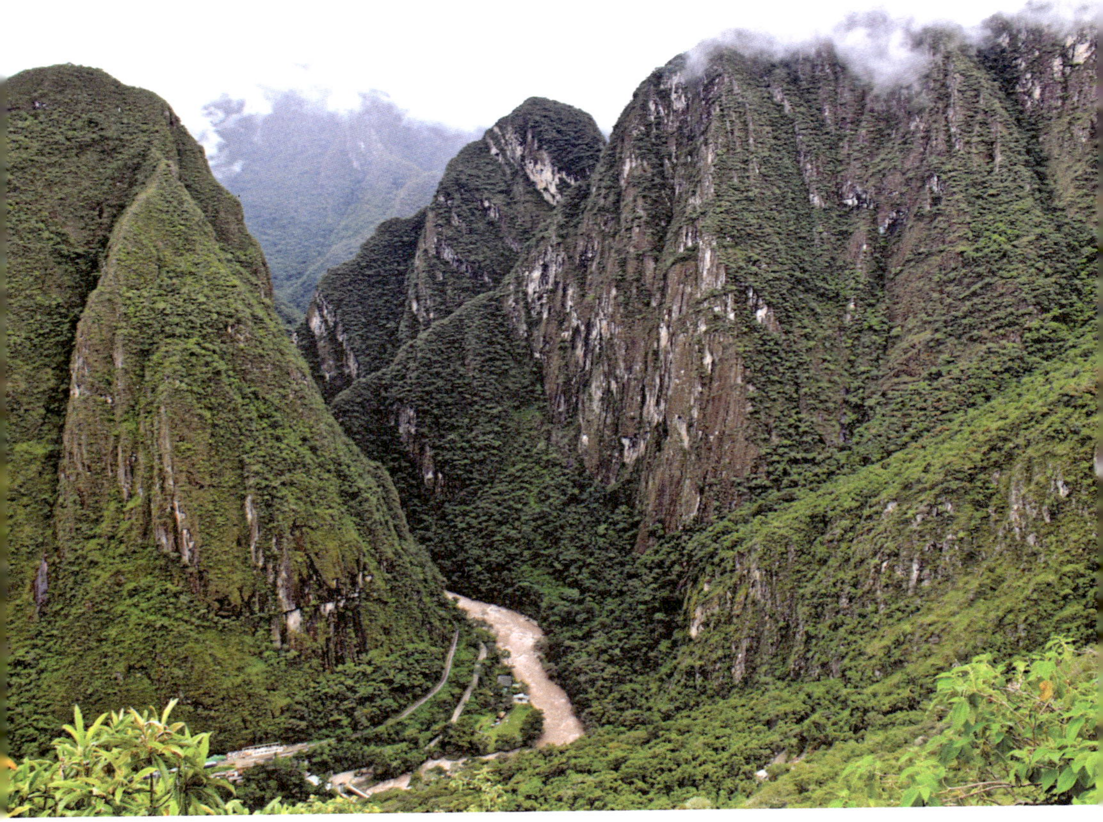

FLANKED BY
PERU'S ANDES MOUNTAIN PEAKS & PLATEAUS

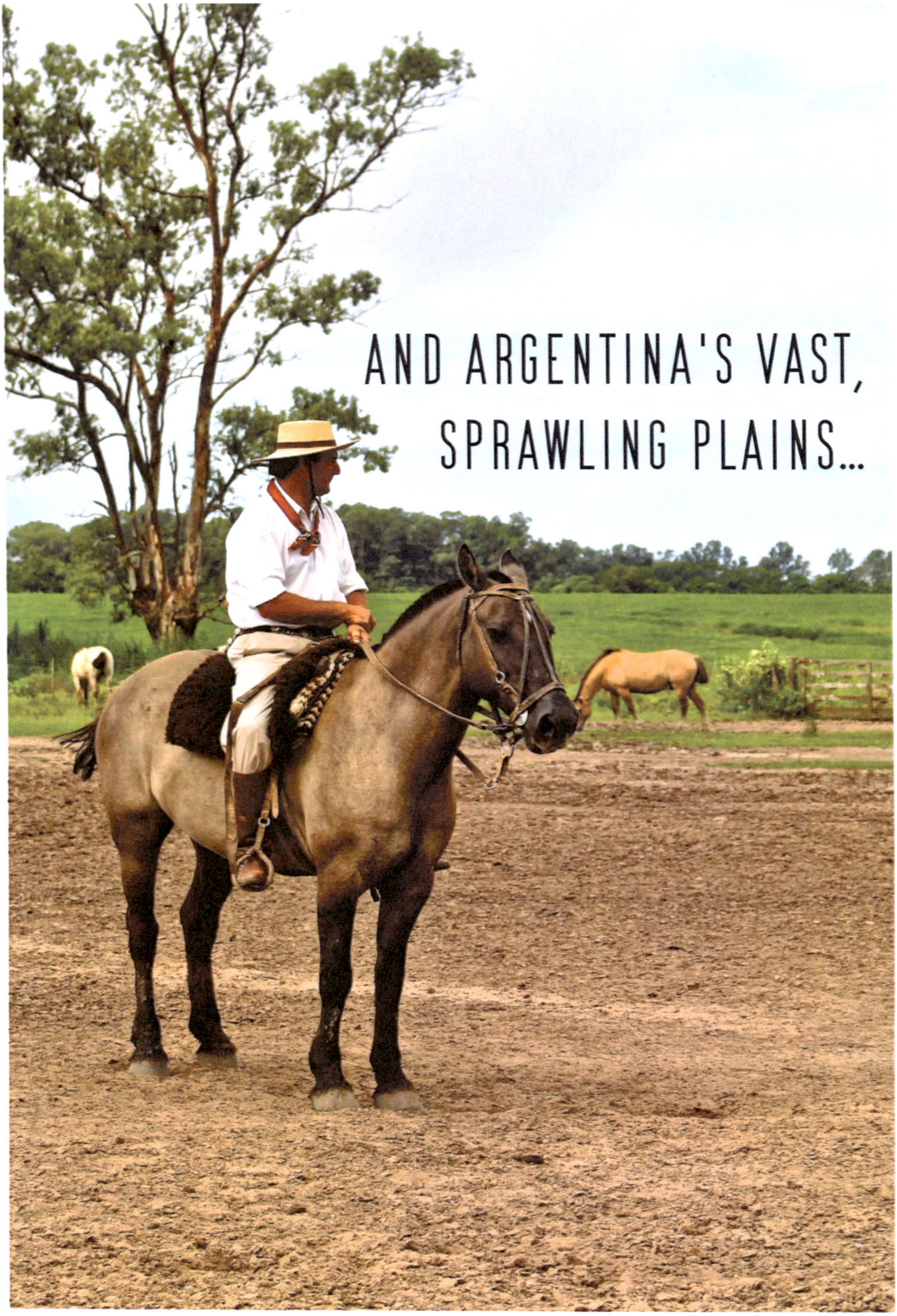
AND ARGENTINA'S VAST,
SPRAWLING PLAINS...

lies the

JEWEL OF THE JOURNEY

Just beyond South America's tip, glistening brighter than any gem, is the seventh continent...

ANTARCTICA

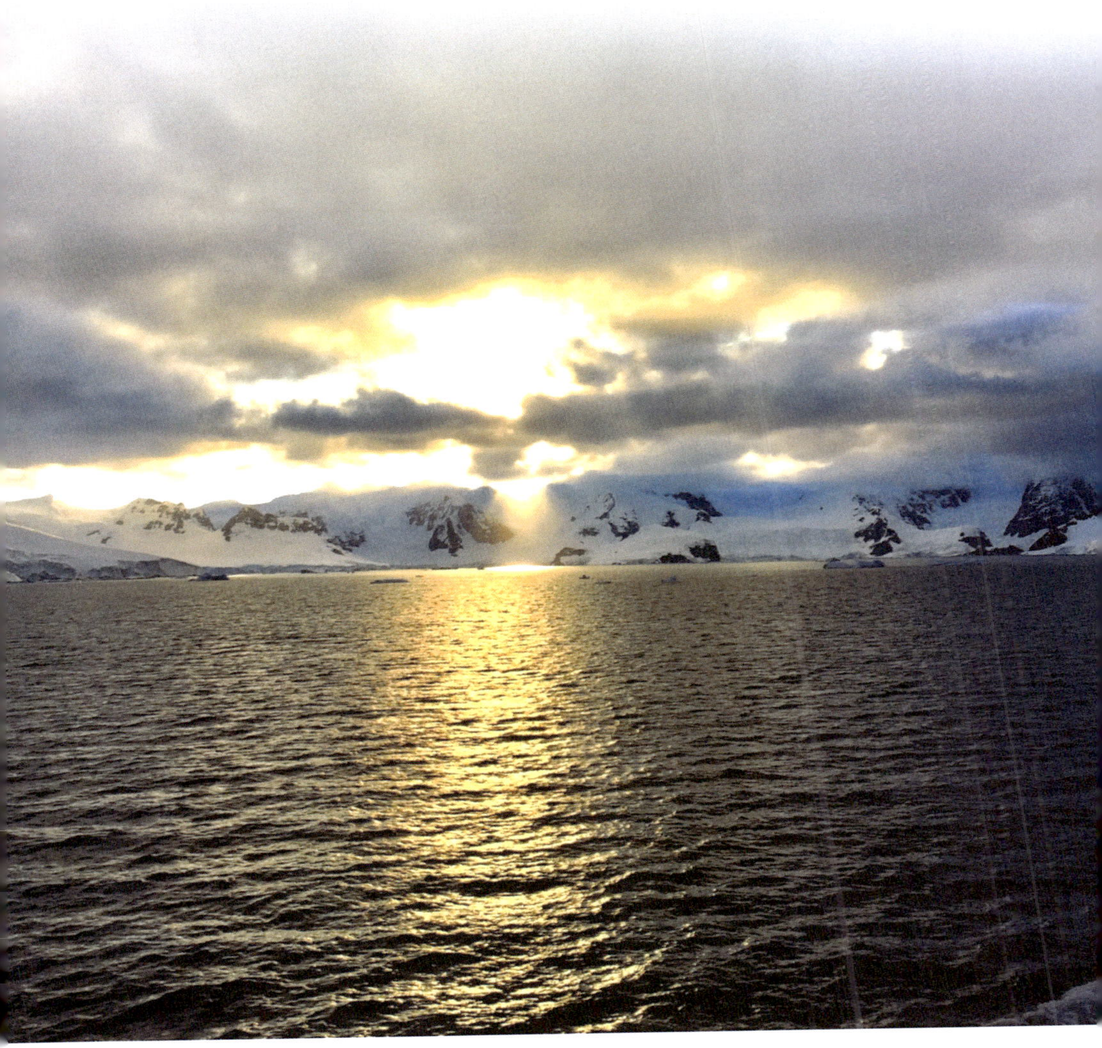

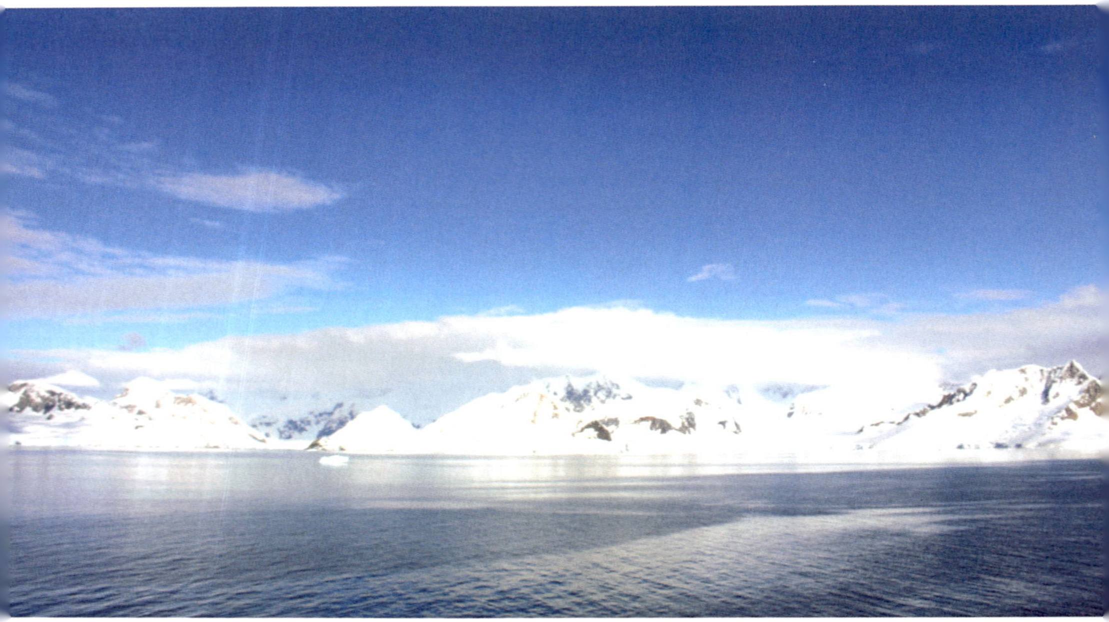

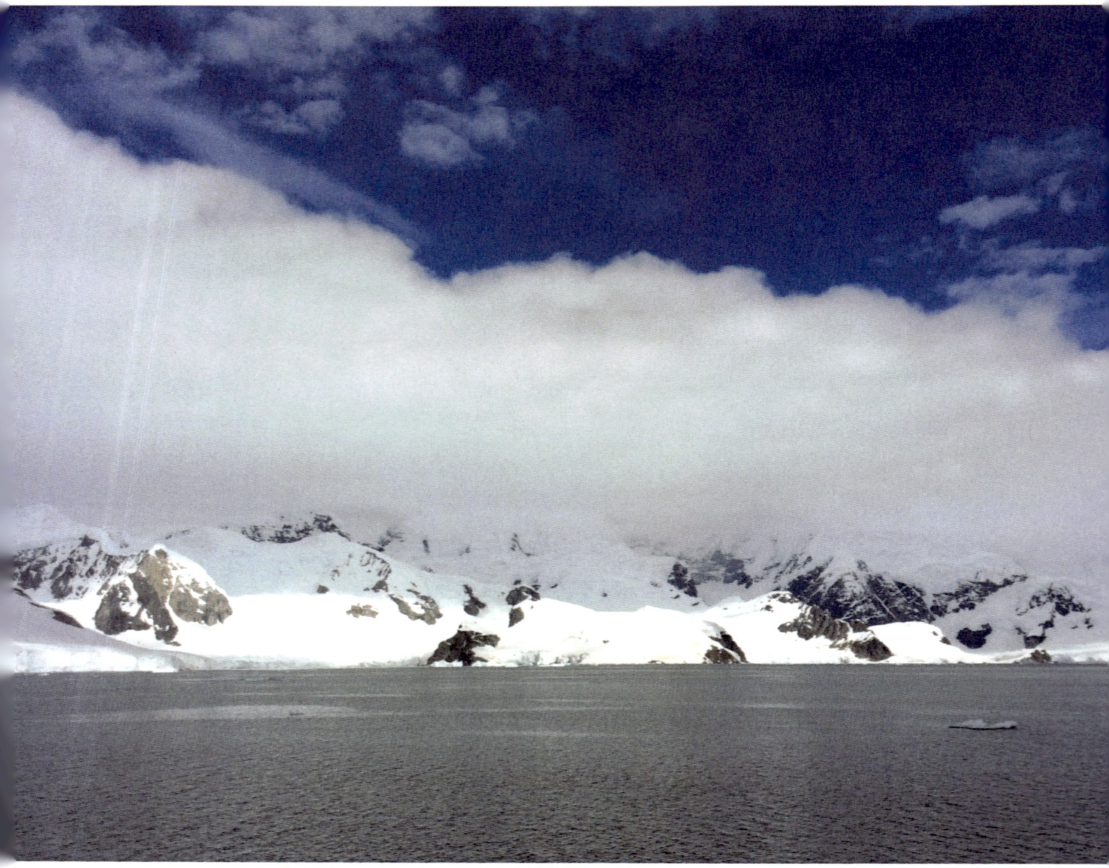

The journey began with a flight to the coastal capital city of Lima, Peru, where land and sea,

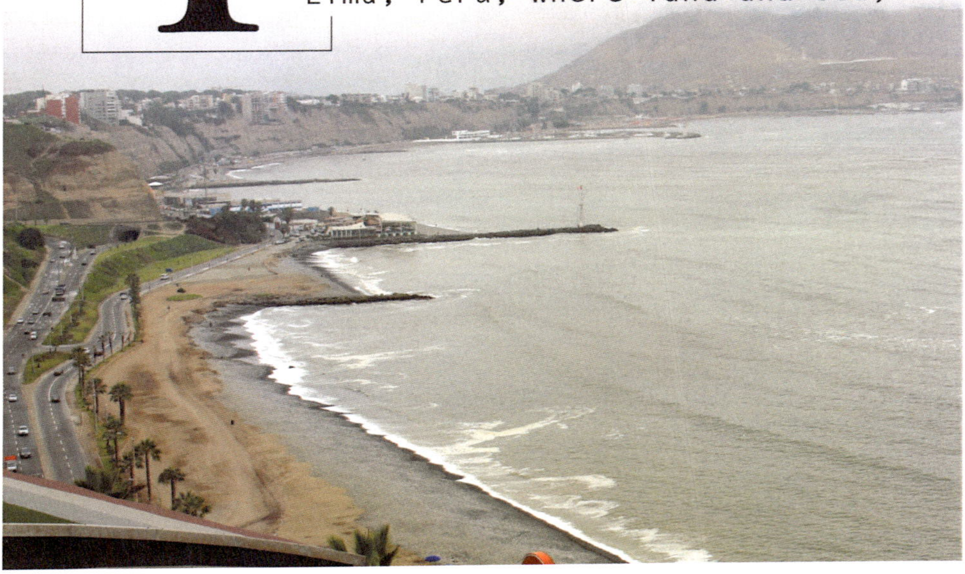

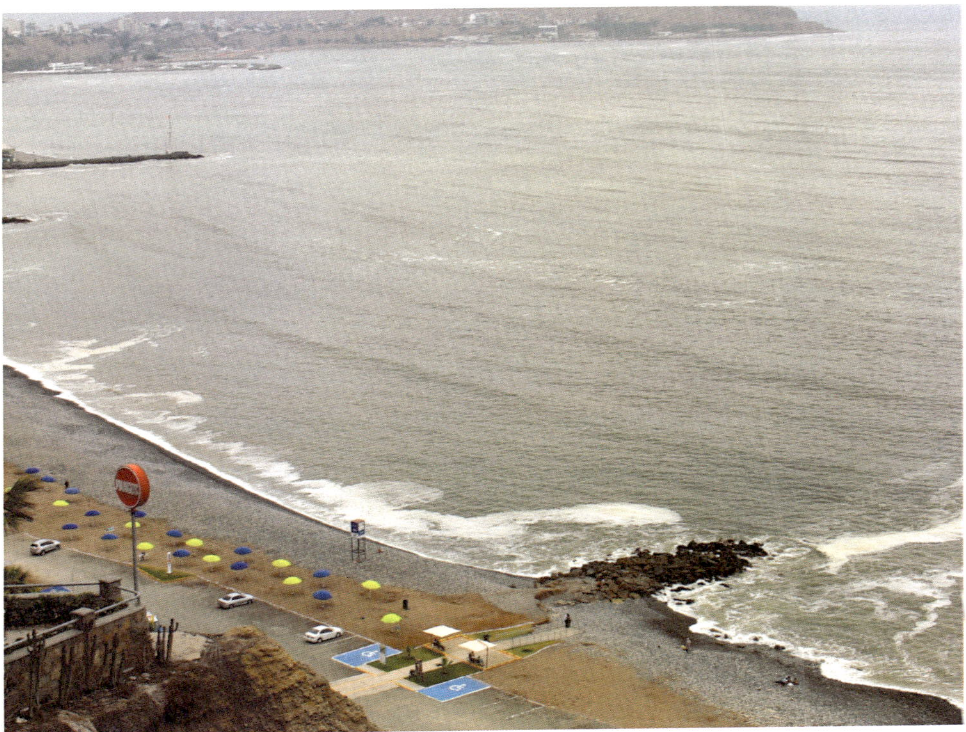

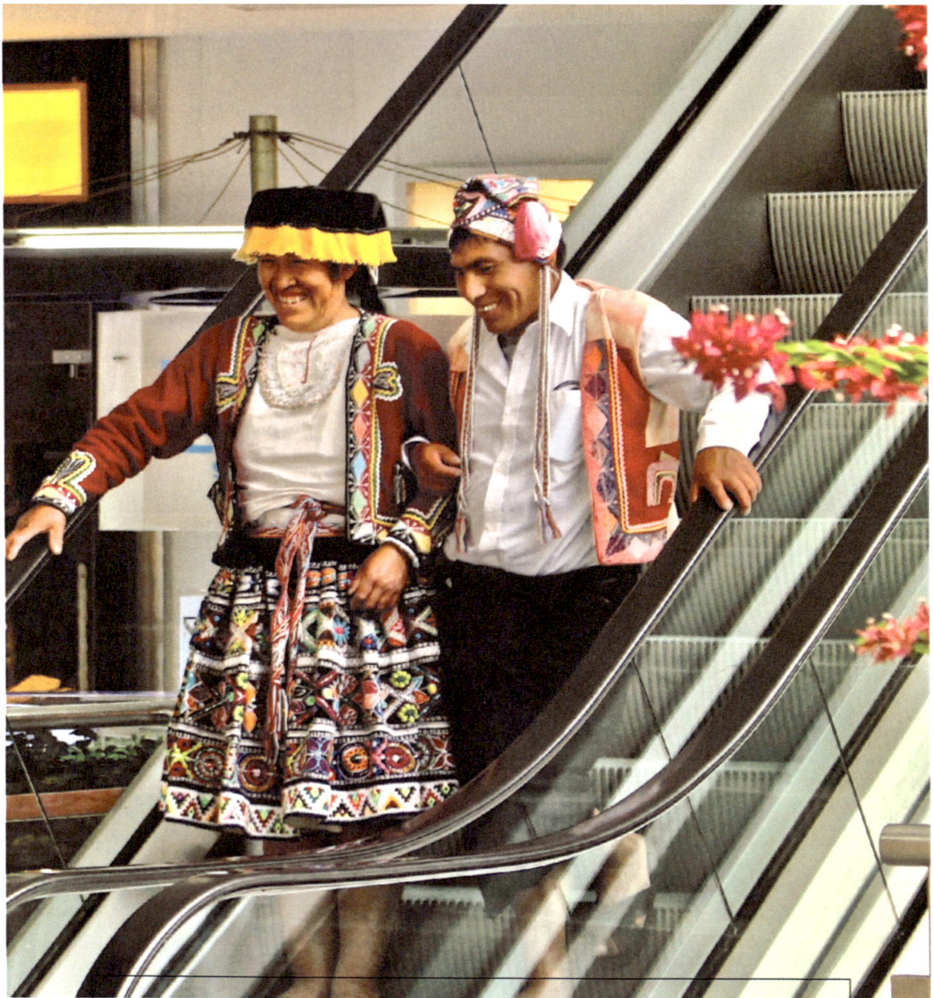

...PAST AND PRESENT, THRIVE IN CO-EXISTENCE.

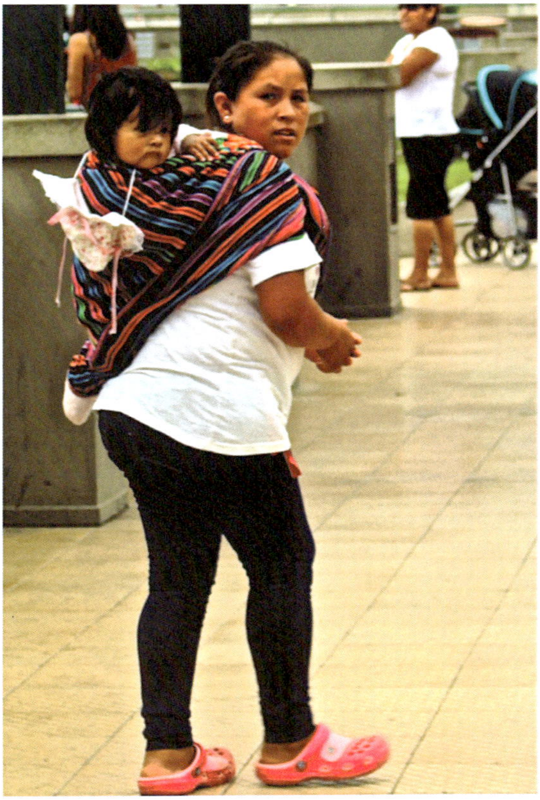

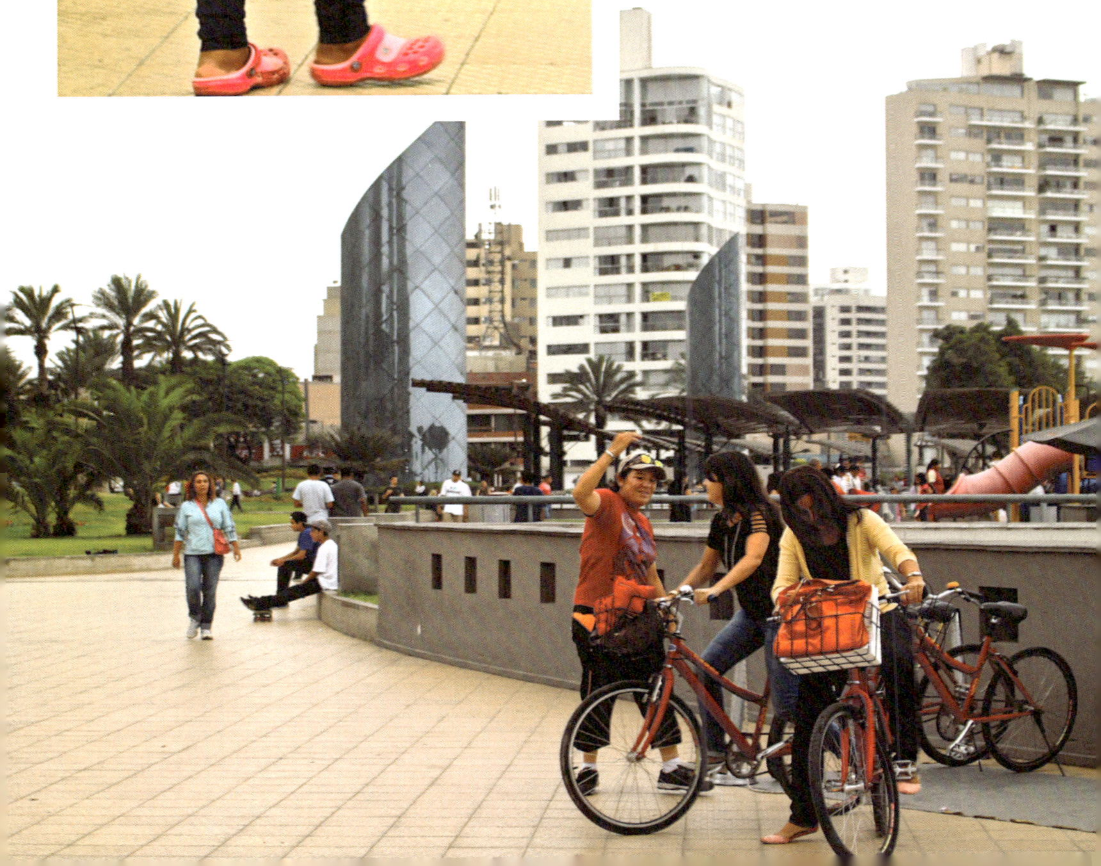

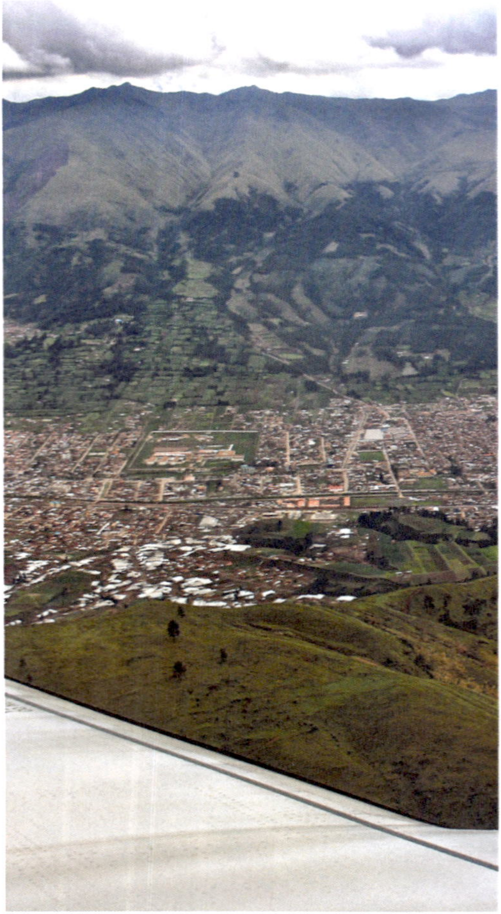

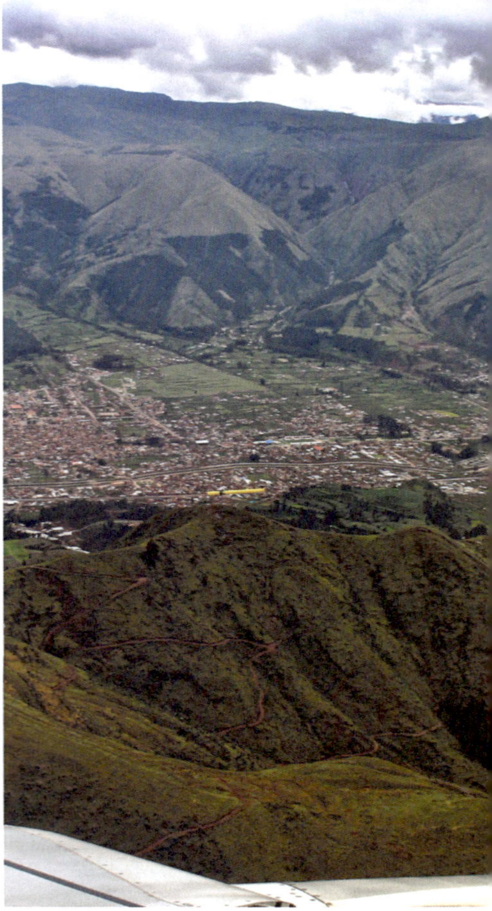

Cuzco,

situated in a valley high in the Peruvian Andes, once capital of the Inca Empire...

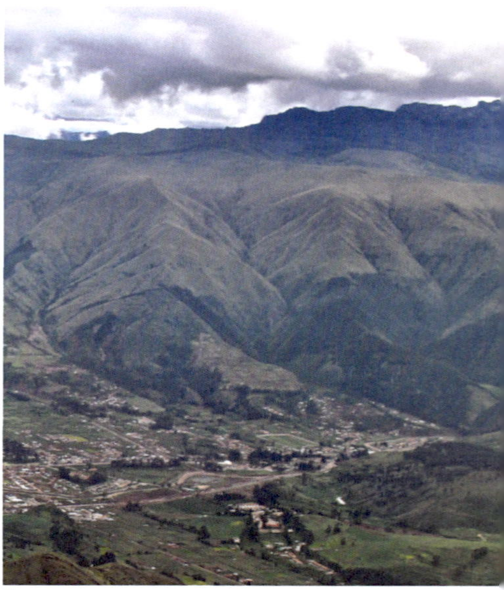

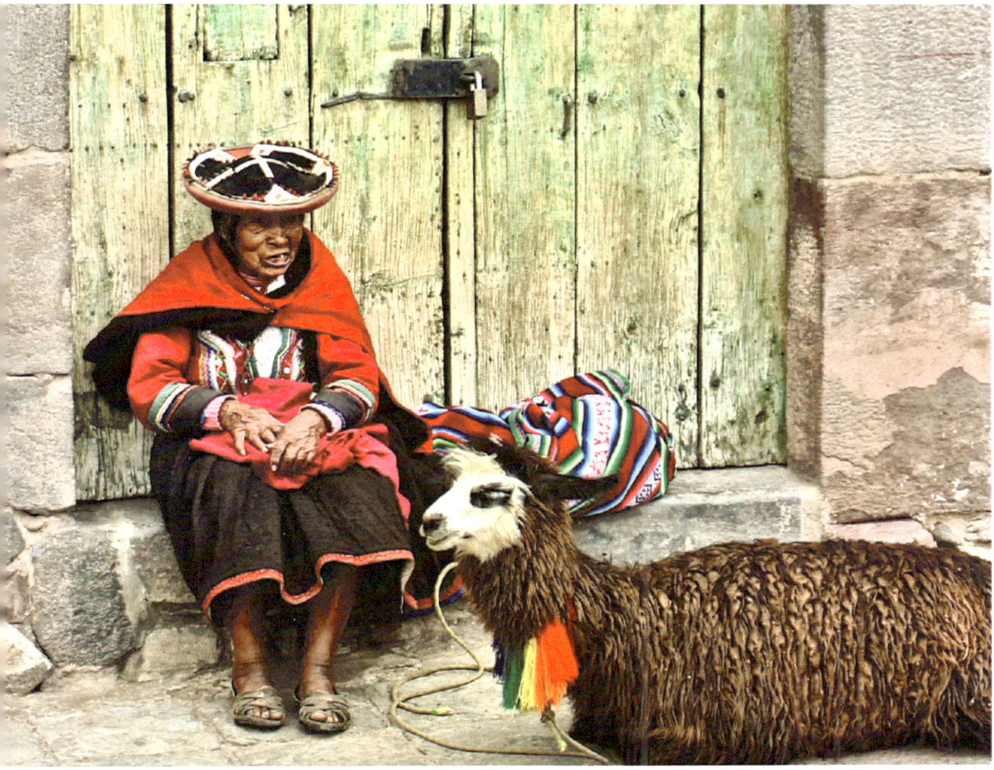

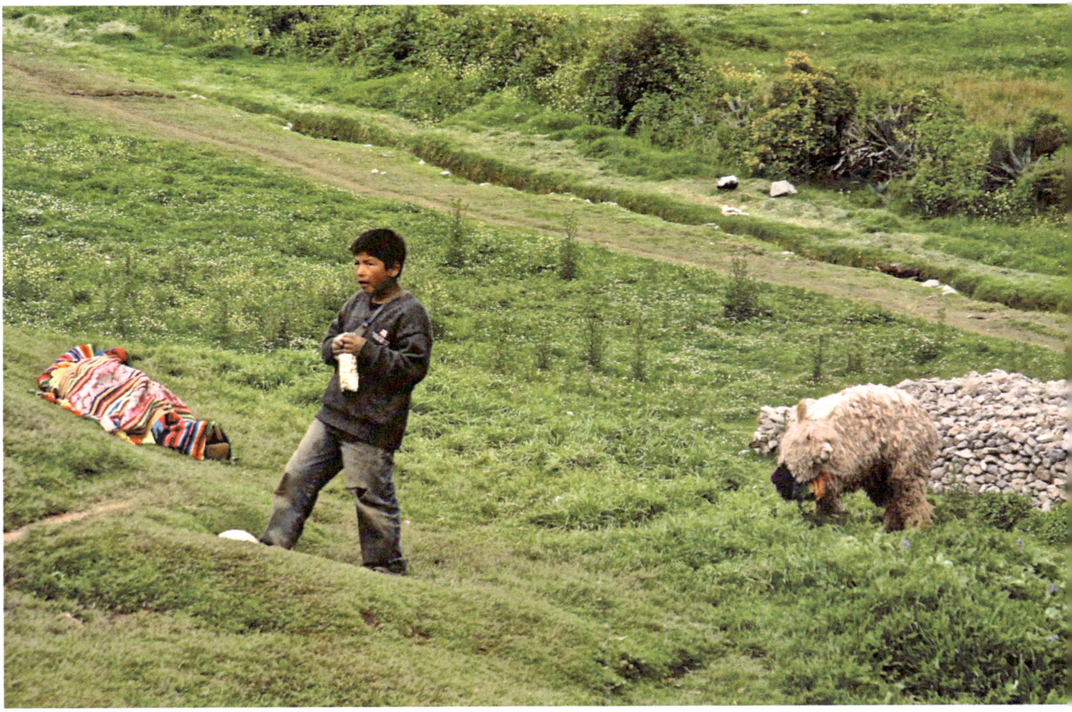

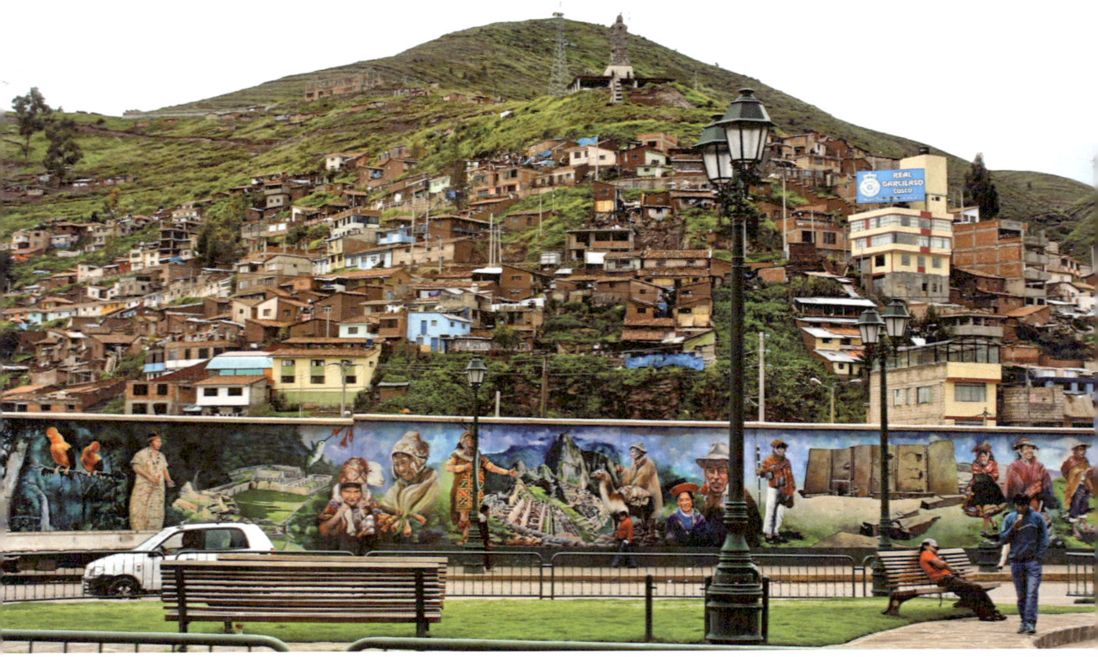

is the doorway to the citadel of

MACHU PICCHU

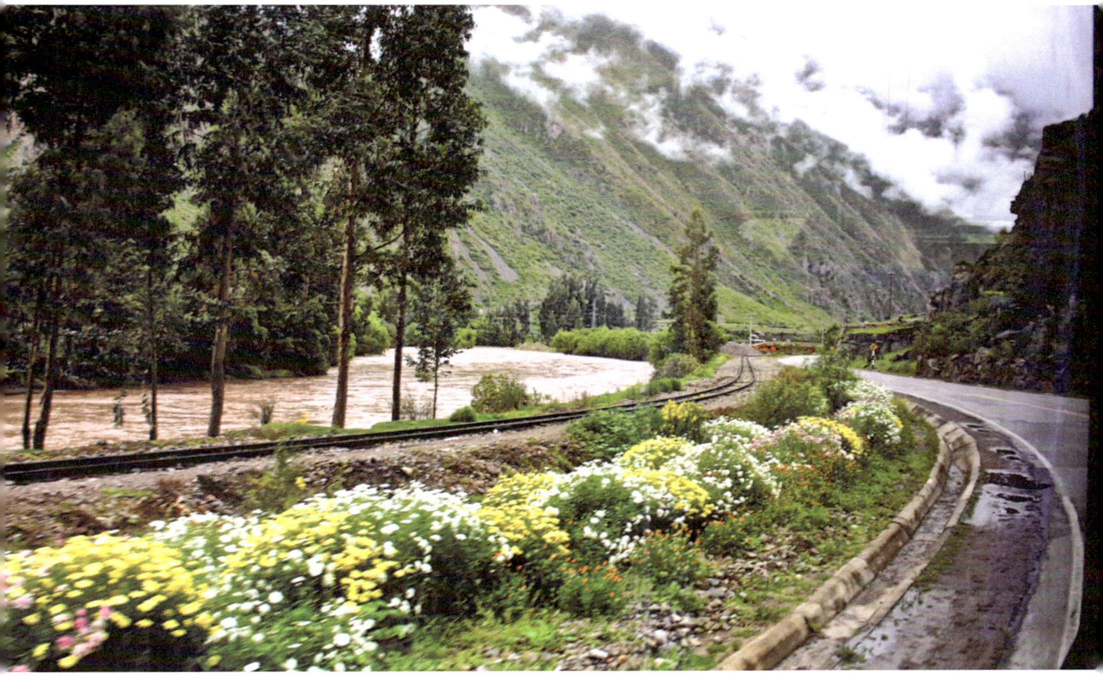

A PANORAMIC TRAIN RIDE...

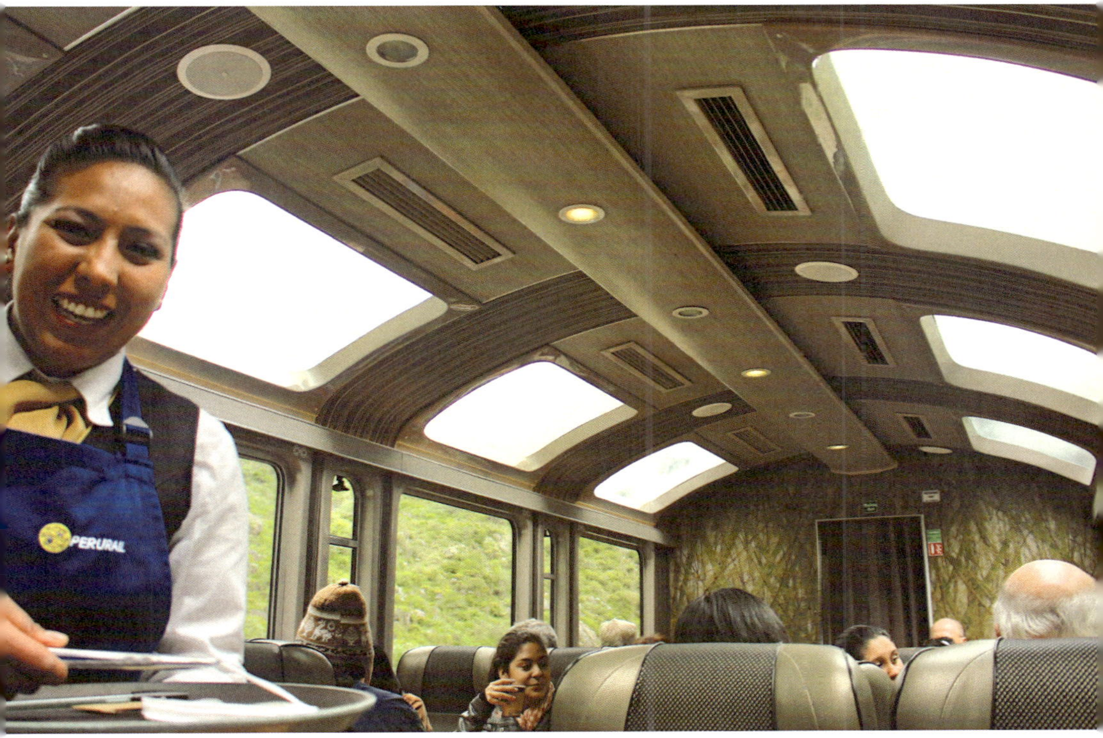

a roughly hewn stairway climb...

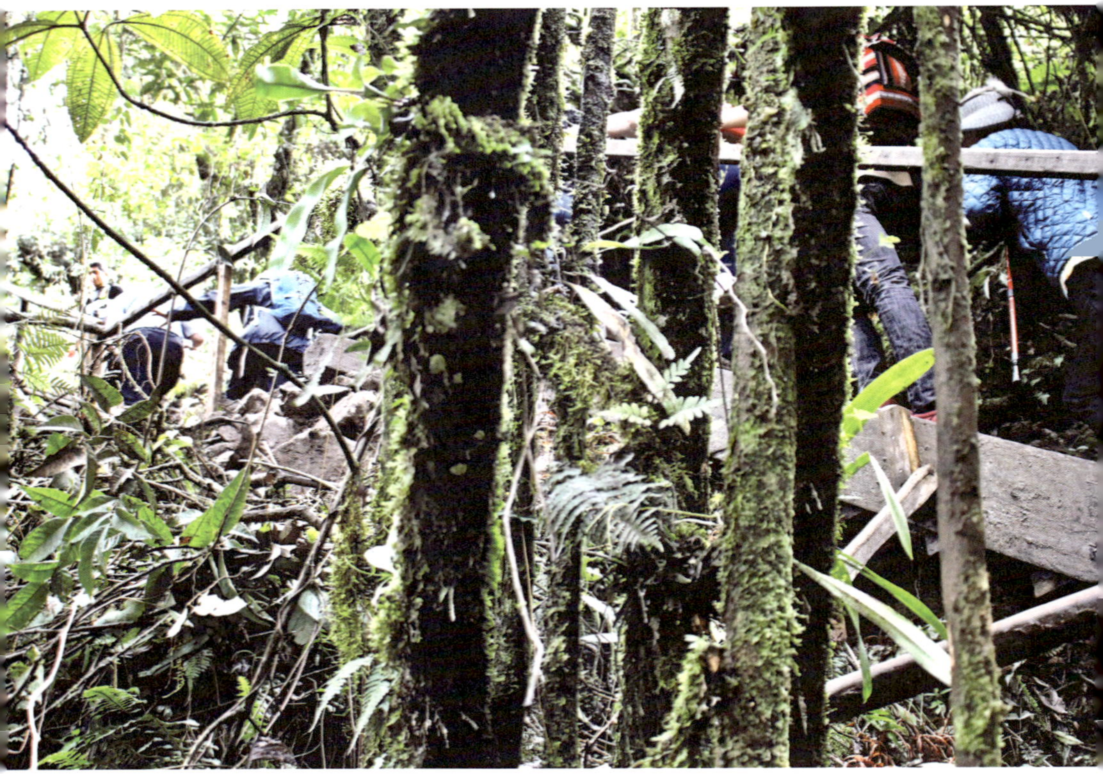

to the wonder of

MACHU PICCHU

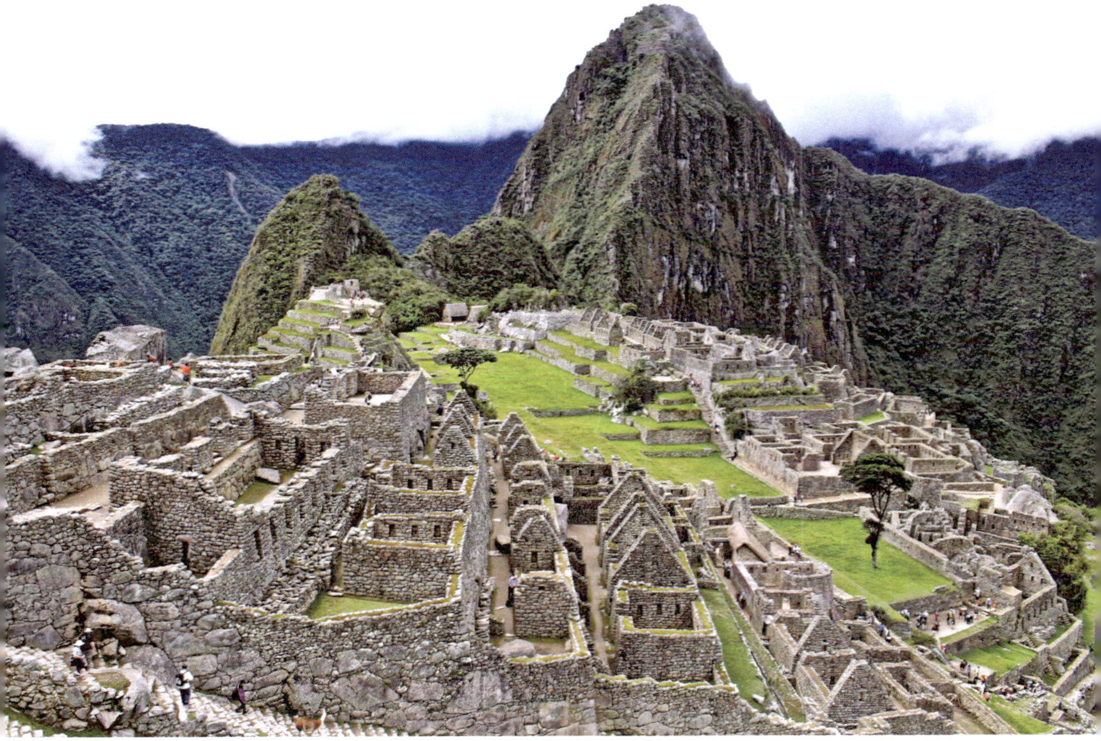

Perched on a high plateau deep in the Amazon jungle and reachable only by train or by foot lies an ancient Incan marvel of mortar-free limestone architecture.

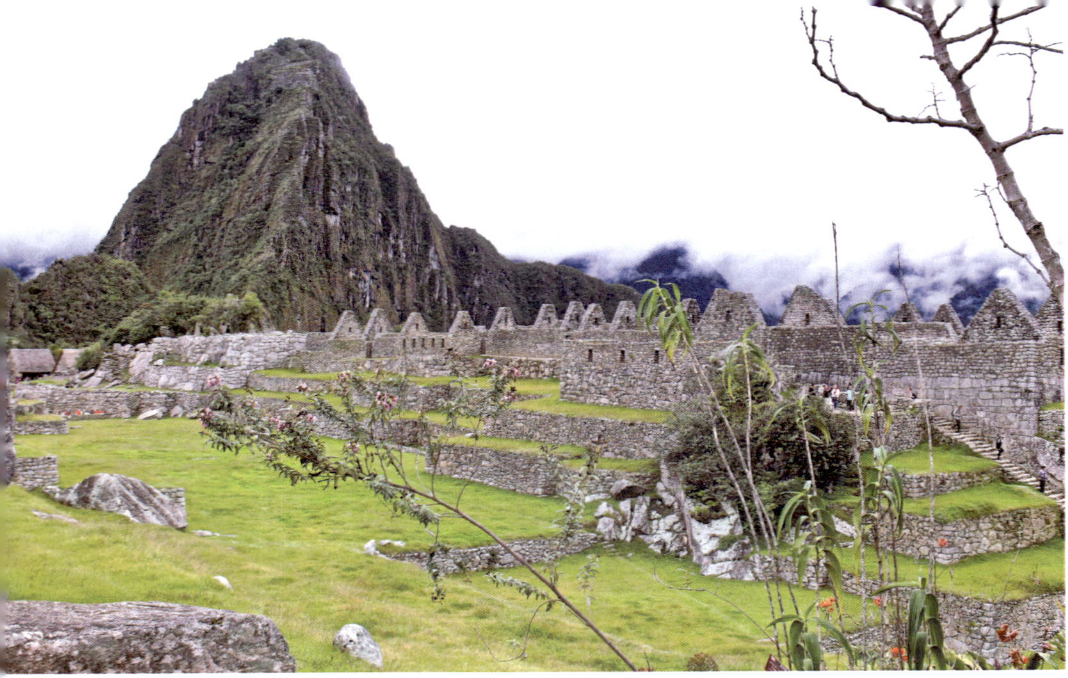

Here,man imitates nature, adapting to the natural form of the mountain, using trapezoidal doors and windows with offset walls to allow for resistance to the seismic activities of the area.

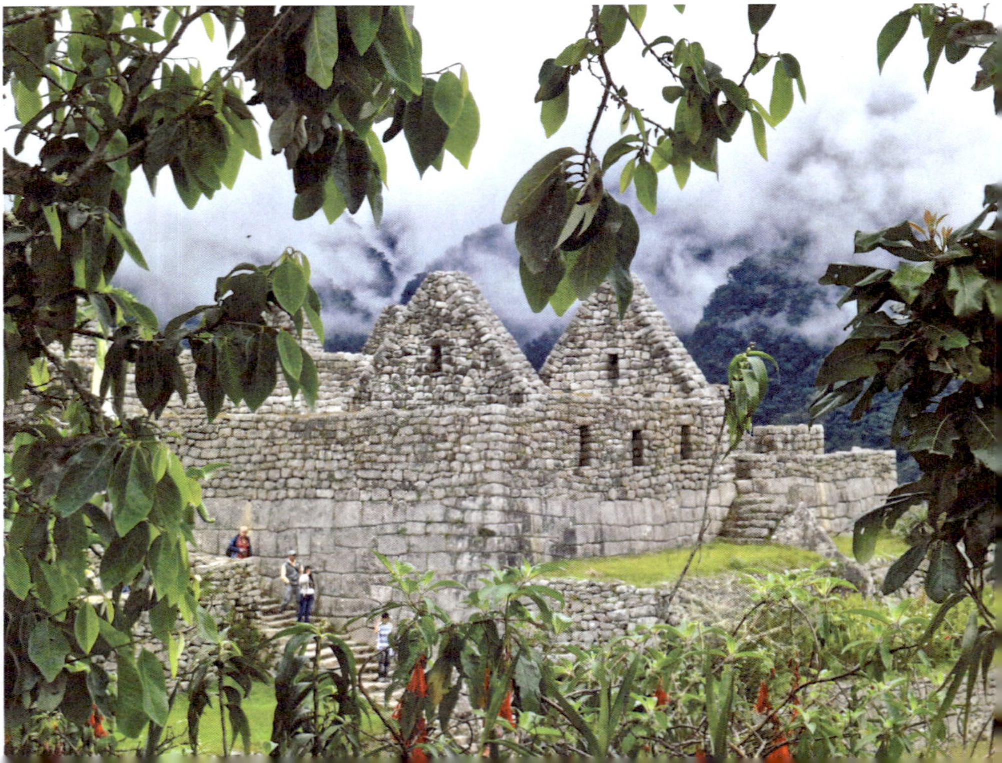

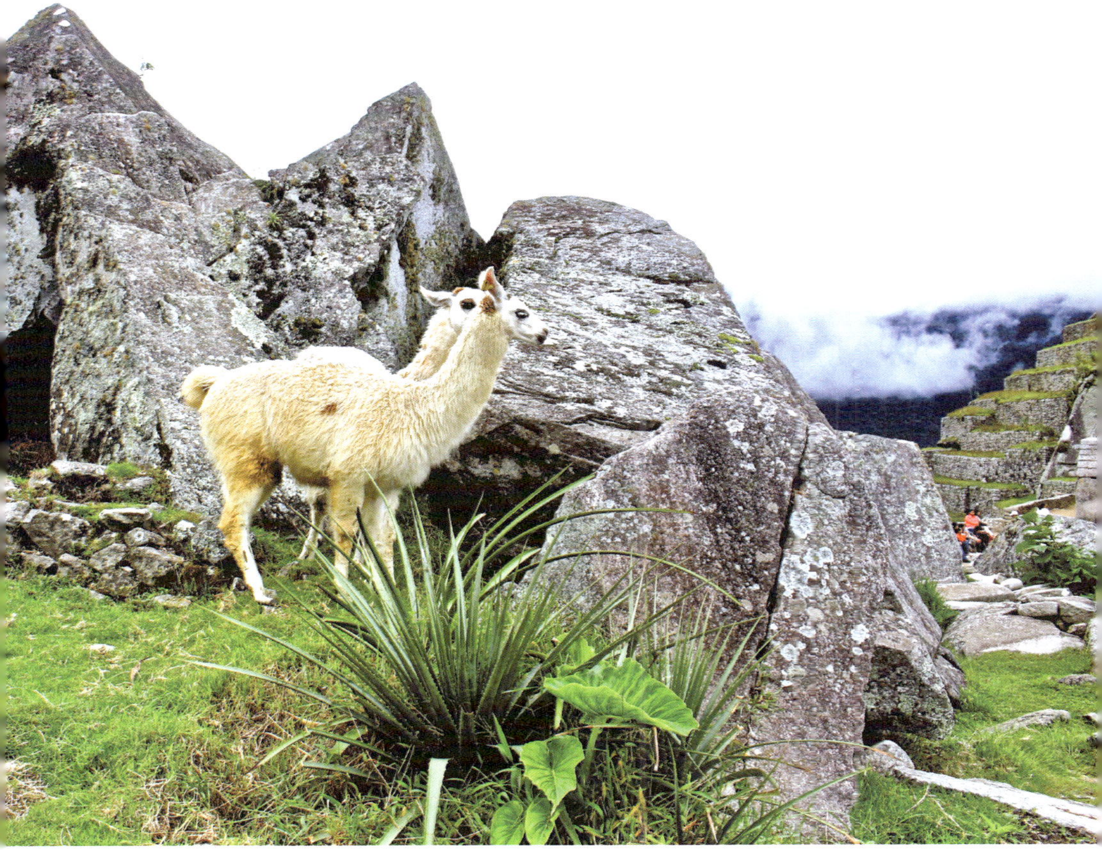

Llamas, played an important role in the development of the Inca Empire.Today these beloved animals captivate the curiosity of visitors.

Machu Picchu's terraces serve as another Inca engineering marvel.These containment constructions prevented land erosion from the rains while the platforms took advantage of the rainwater as an irrigation source.

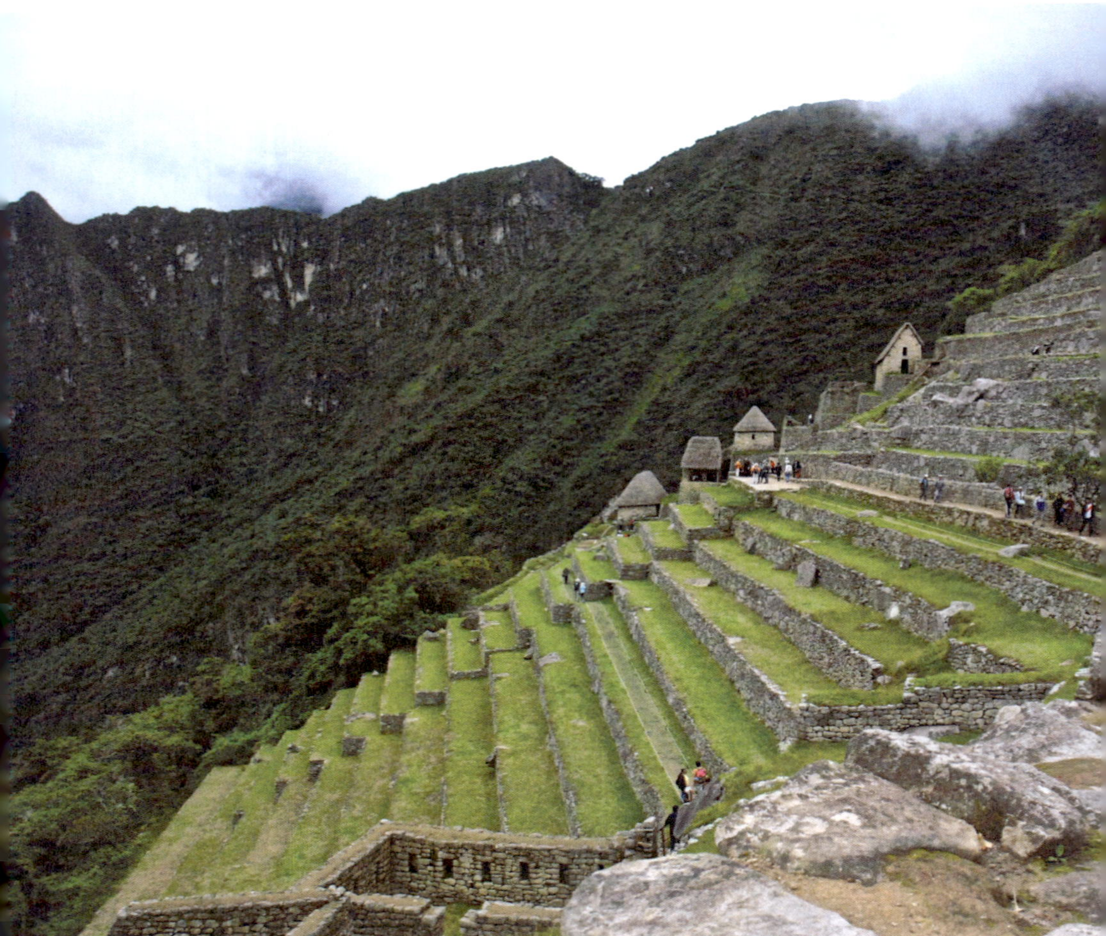

THE JOURNEY SOUTH REVEALS
VASTLY VARYING PLACES, SUCH AS,
THE MODERN METROPOLIS OF VALPARAISO,
CHILE.

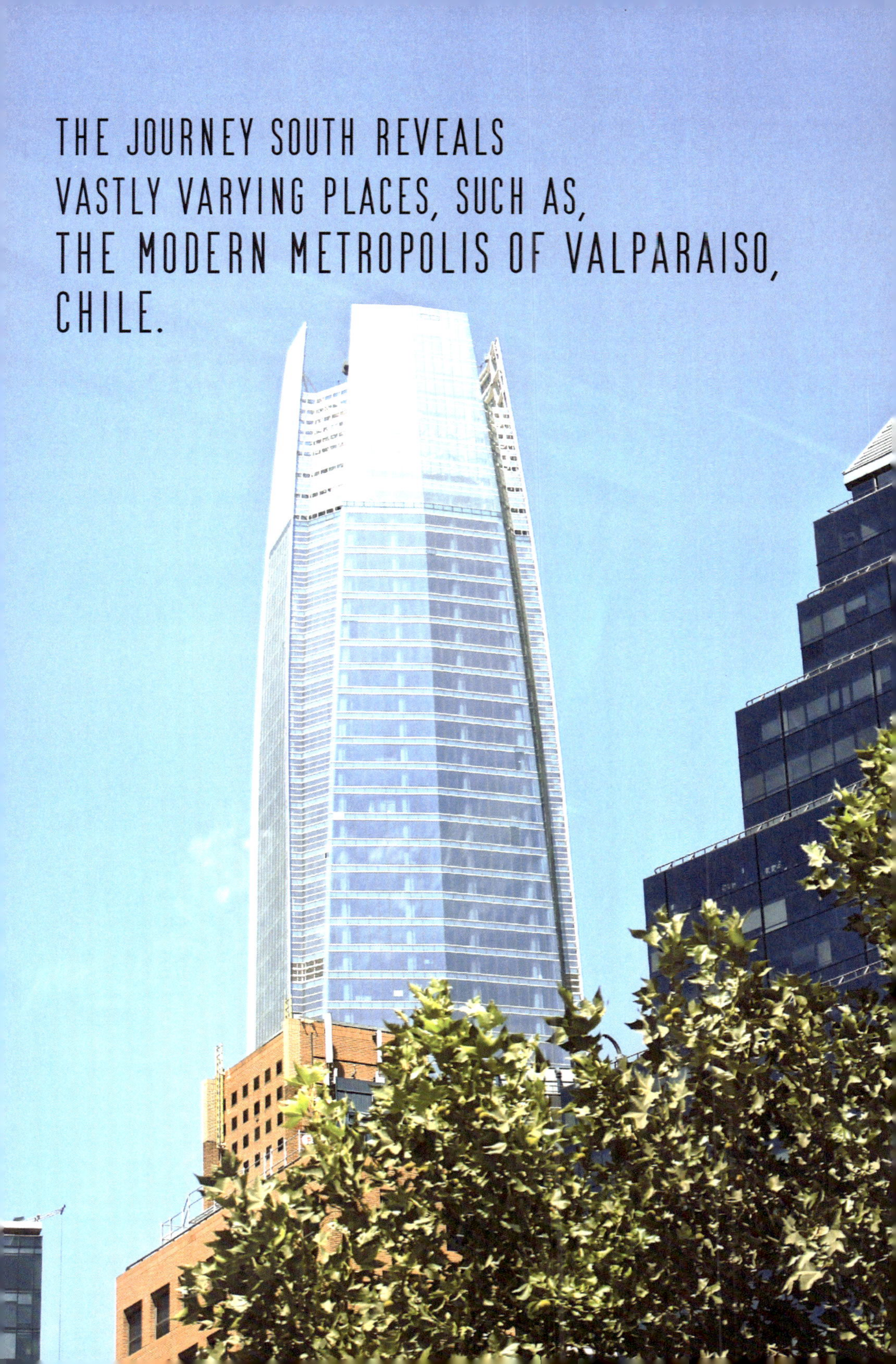

The next

Chilean port is its salmon capital of **Puerto Montt.**

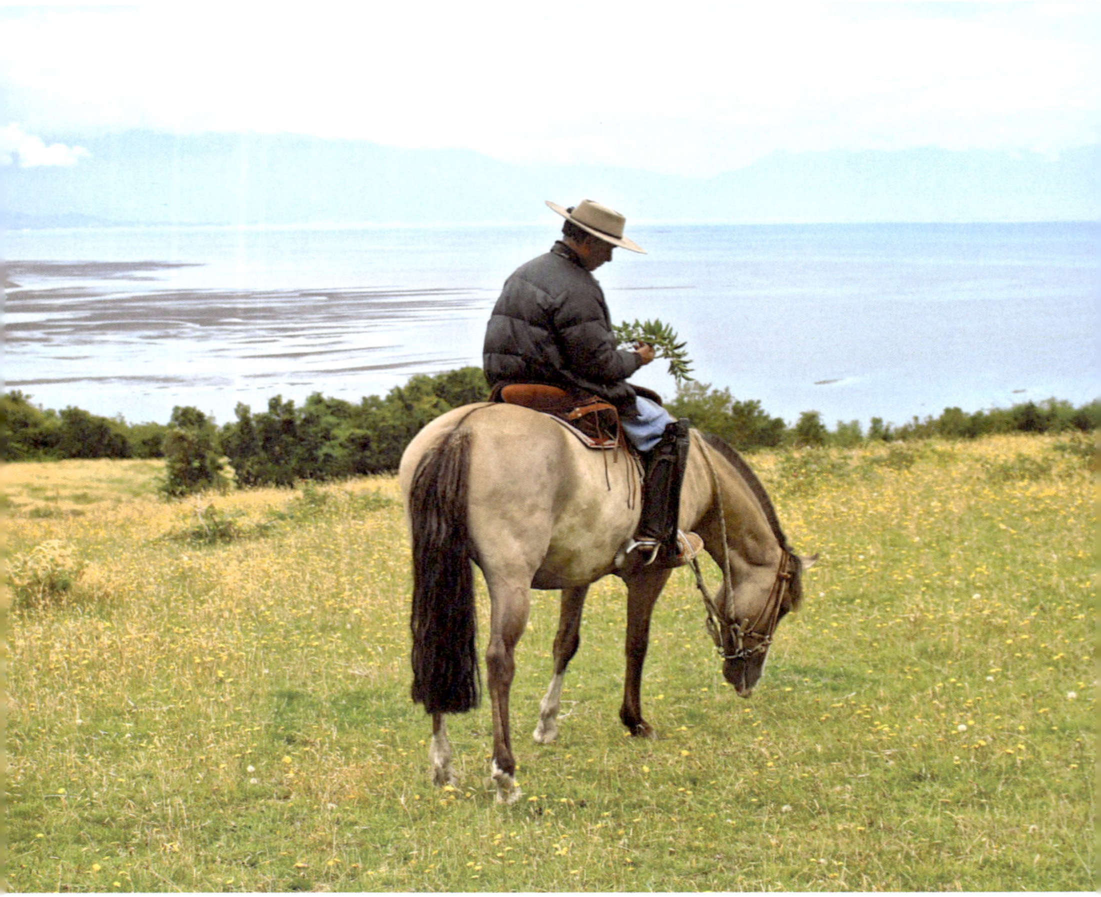

THE CHILEAN COMMUNE OF CASTRO the third oldest city in Chile, is also one of its most colorful.

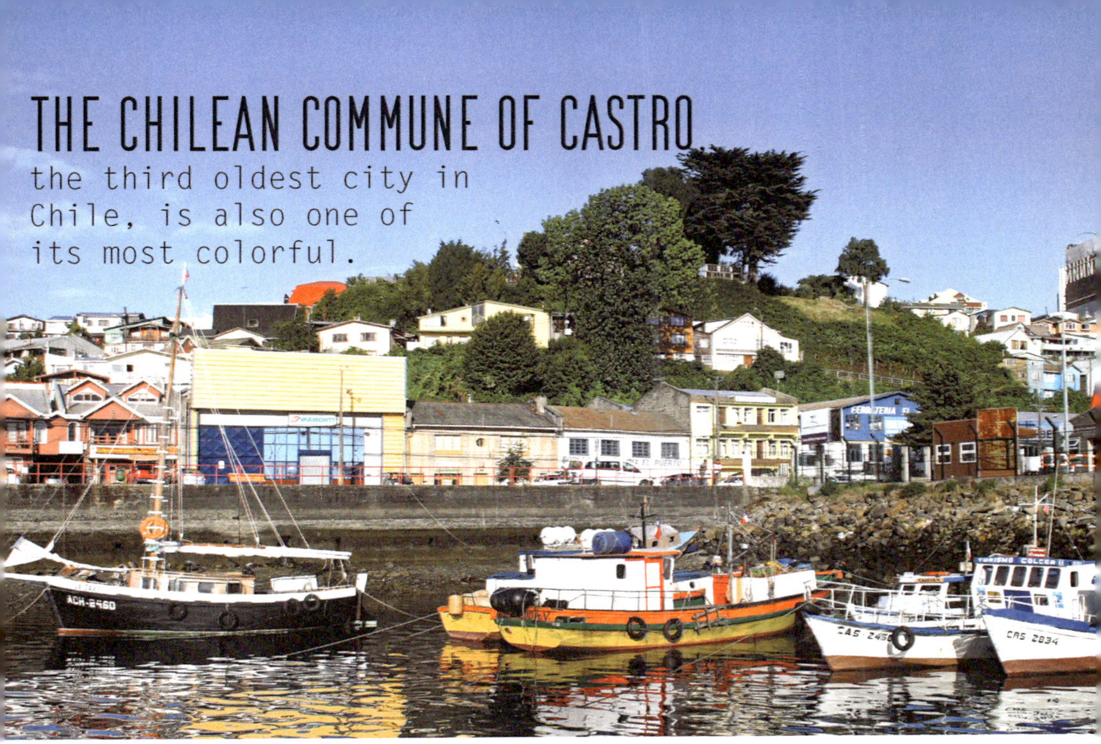

PUERTO CHACABUCO is another main cruise port on the continuing journey south.

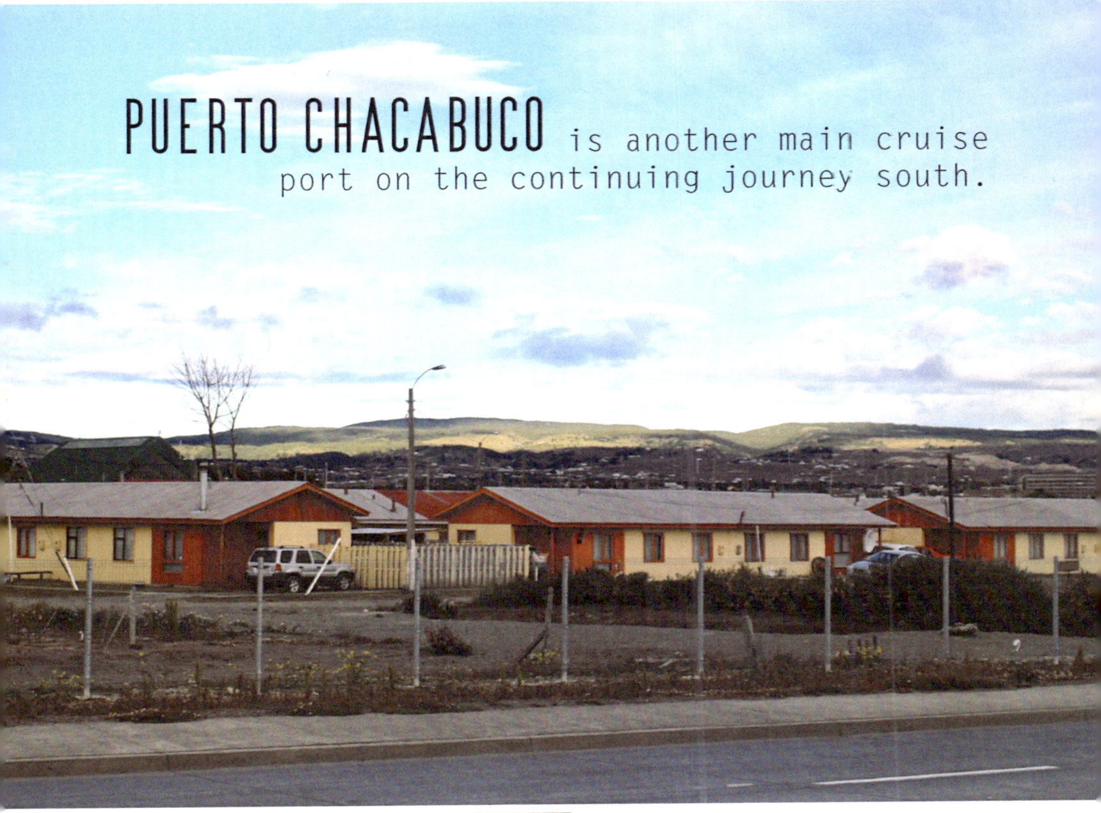

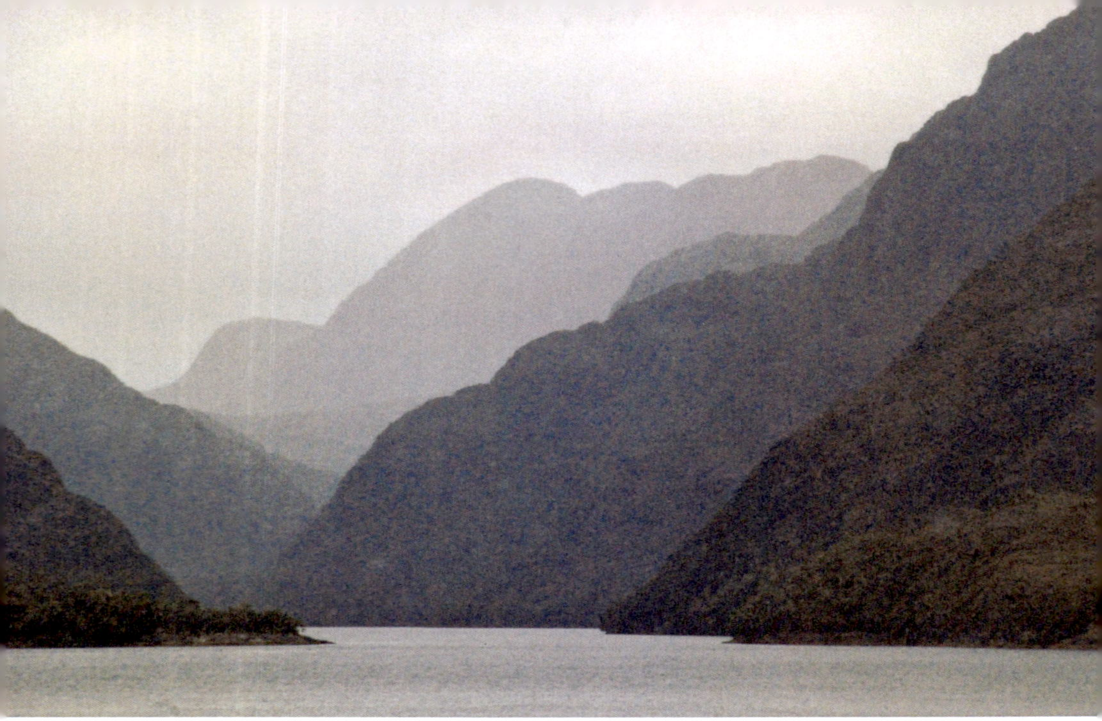

A scarcely explored region, SOUTHERN CHILE'S FJORDS stand majestically with rugged mountains and glacier-covered valleys.

The thick ice floes of the Two-mile wide AMALIA GLACIER set it apart as it plunges into the sea

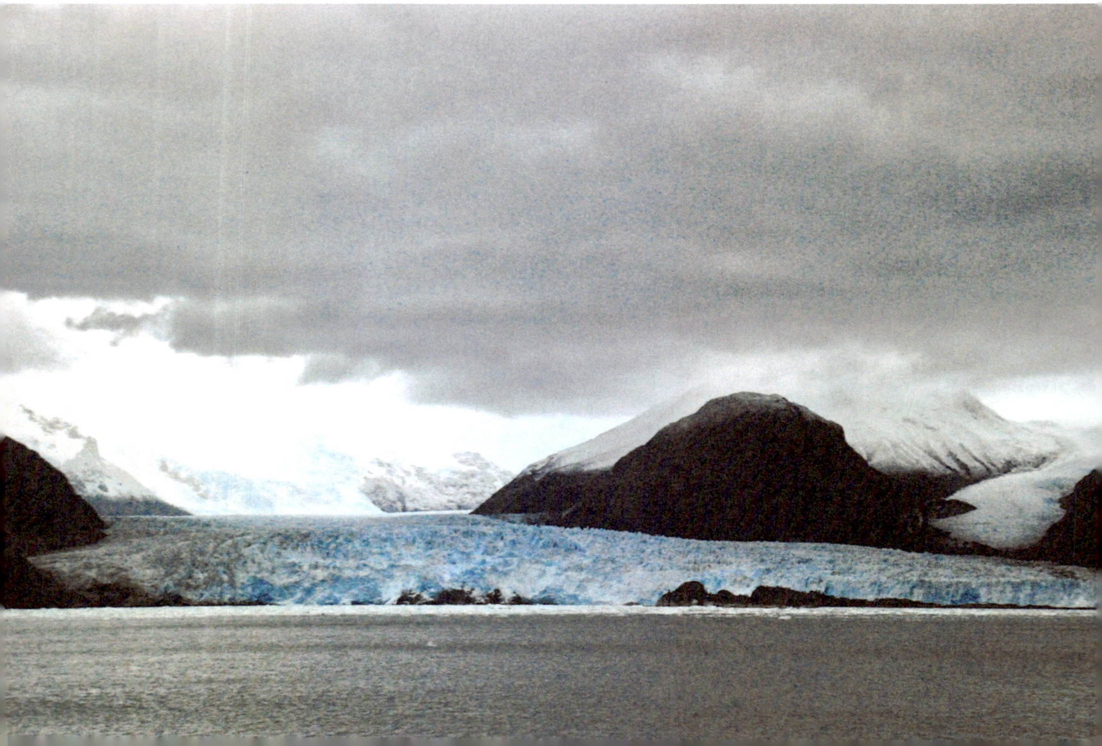

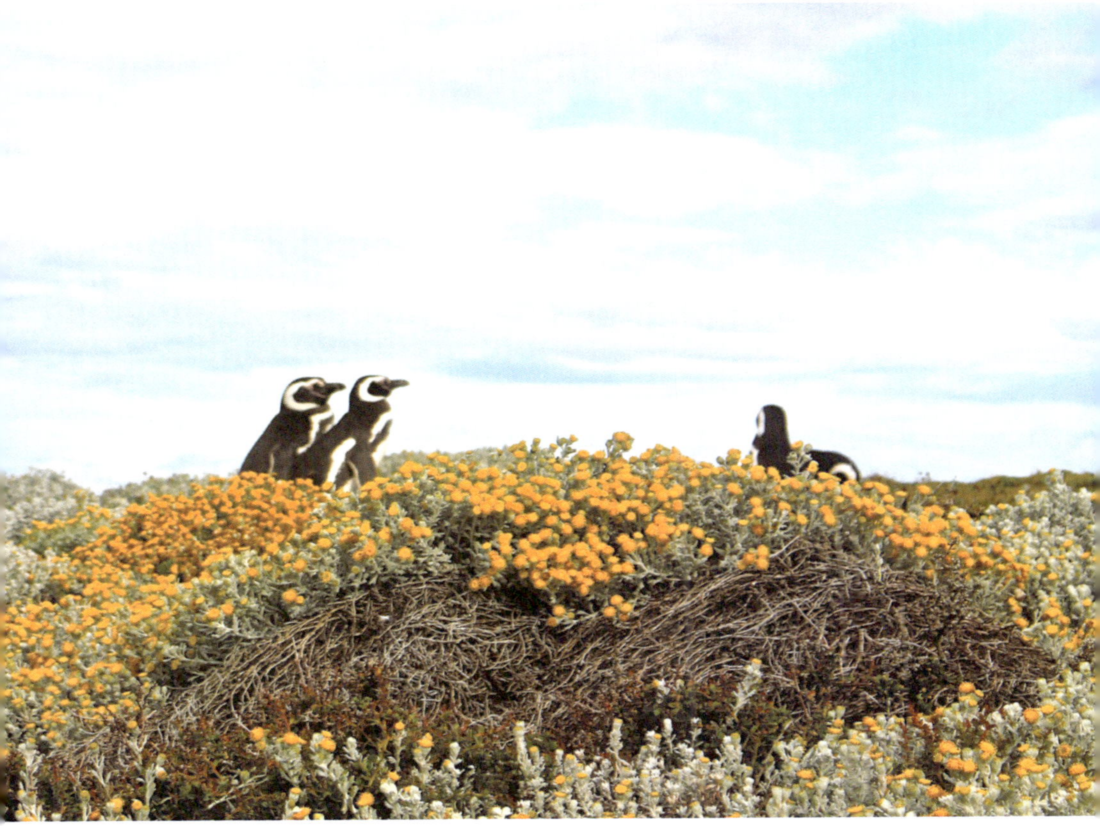

PUNTA ARENAS,

the capital of the Southern Region, zealously promotes and protects a nearby national monument rookery of around **120,000 penguins**.

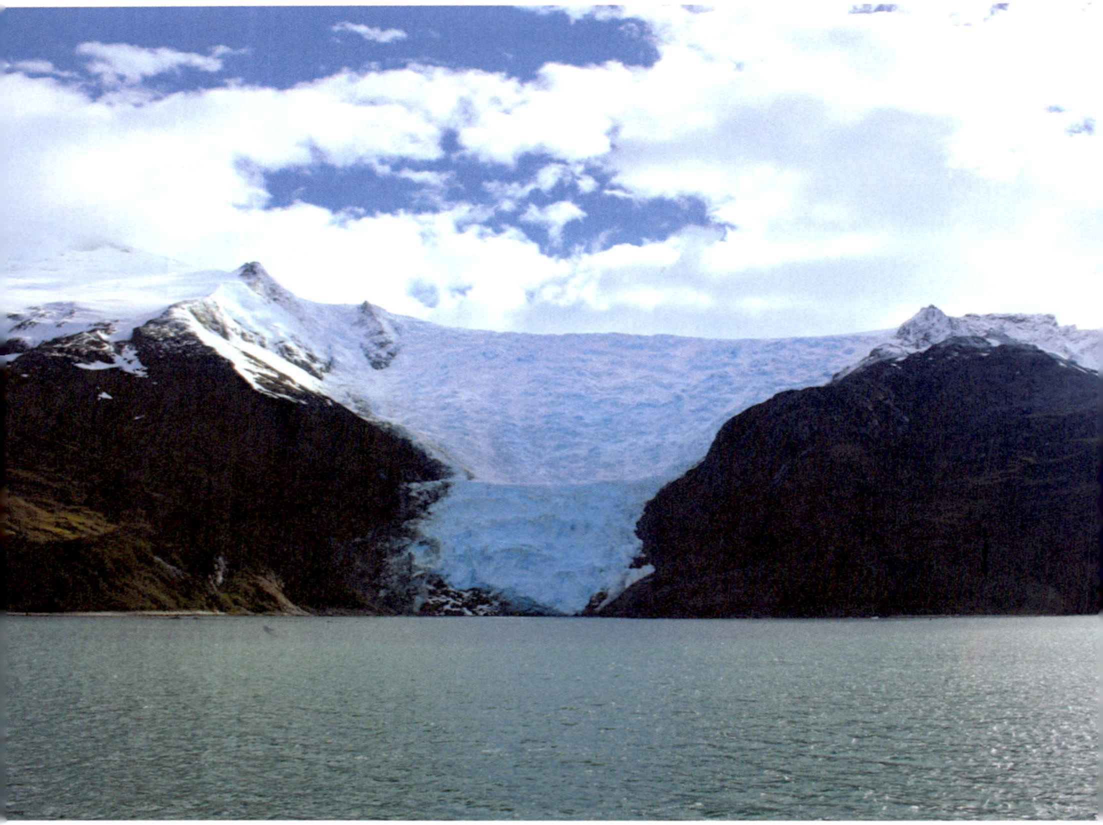

The unmatched frozen beauty of

GLACIER ALLEY

is the opening introduction to the inexplicable splendor that lies ahead.

Continuing down South America's western ccast-line ultimately reveals the southernmcst city in the world, the colorful capital city of

TIERRA DEL FUEGO PROVINCE, USHUAIA, ARGENTINA.

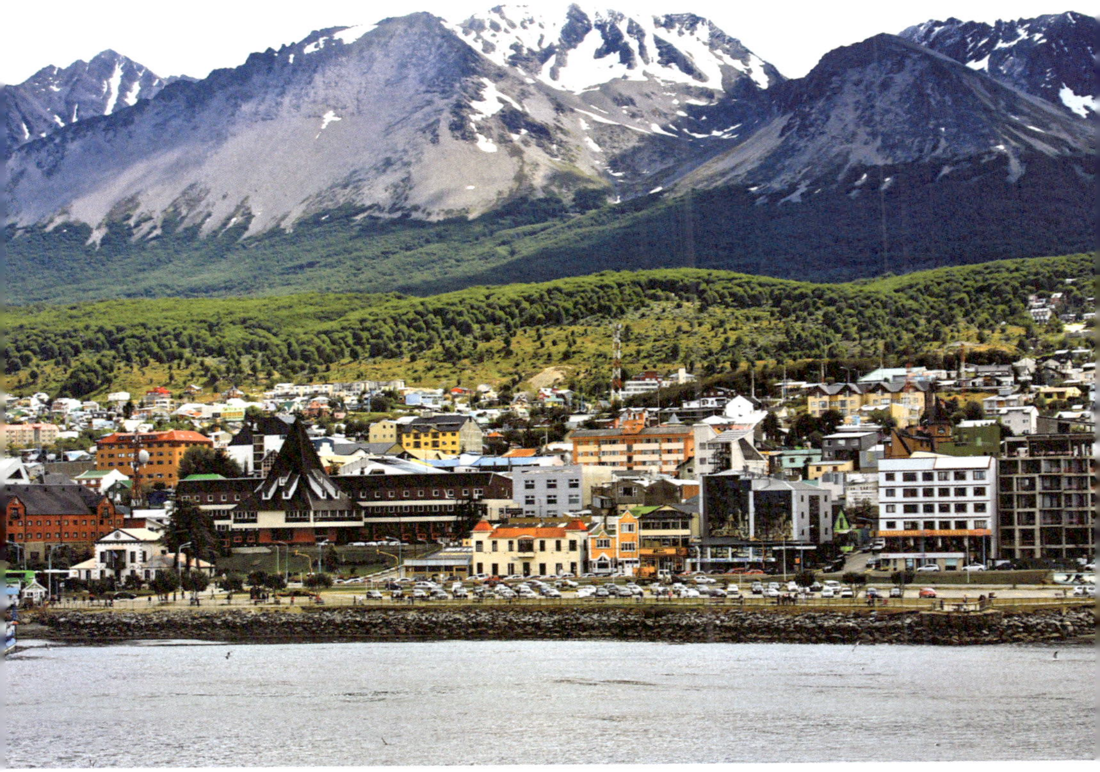

The pride of USHUAIA:

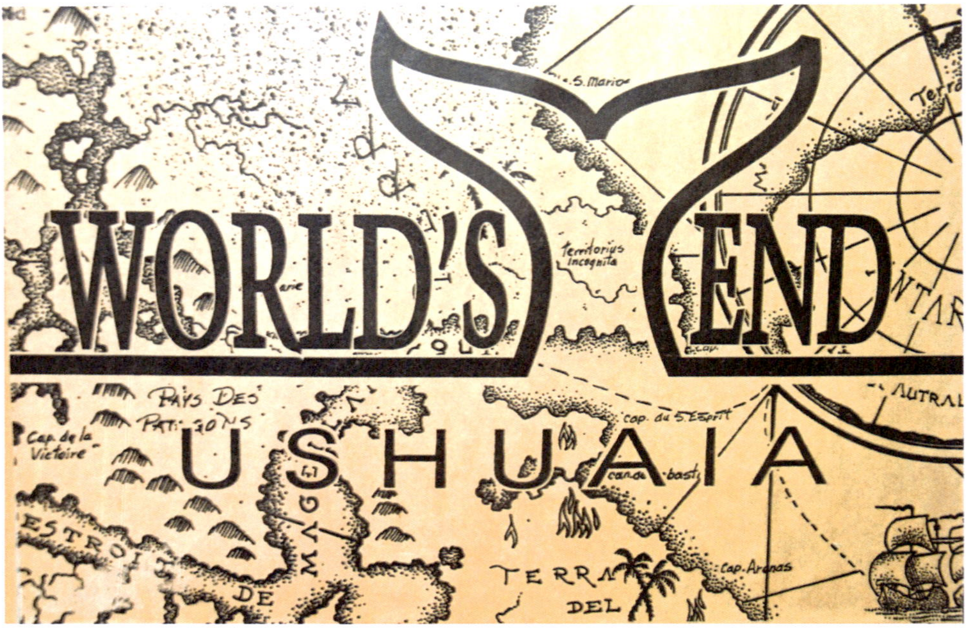

Morning reveals...

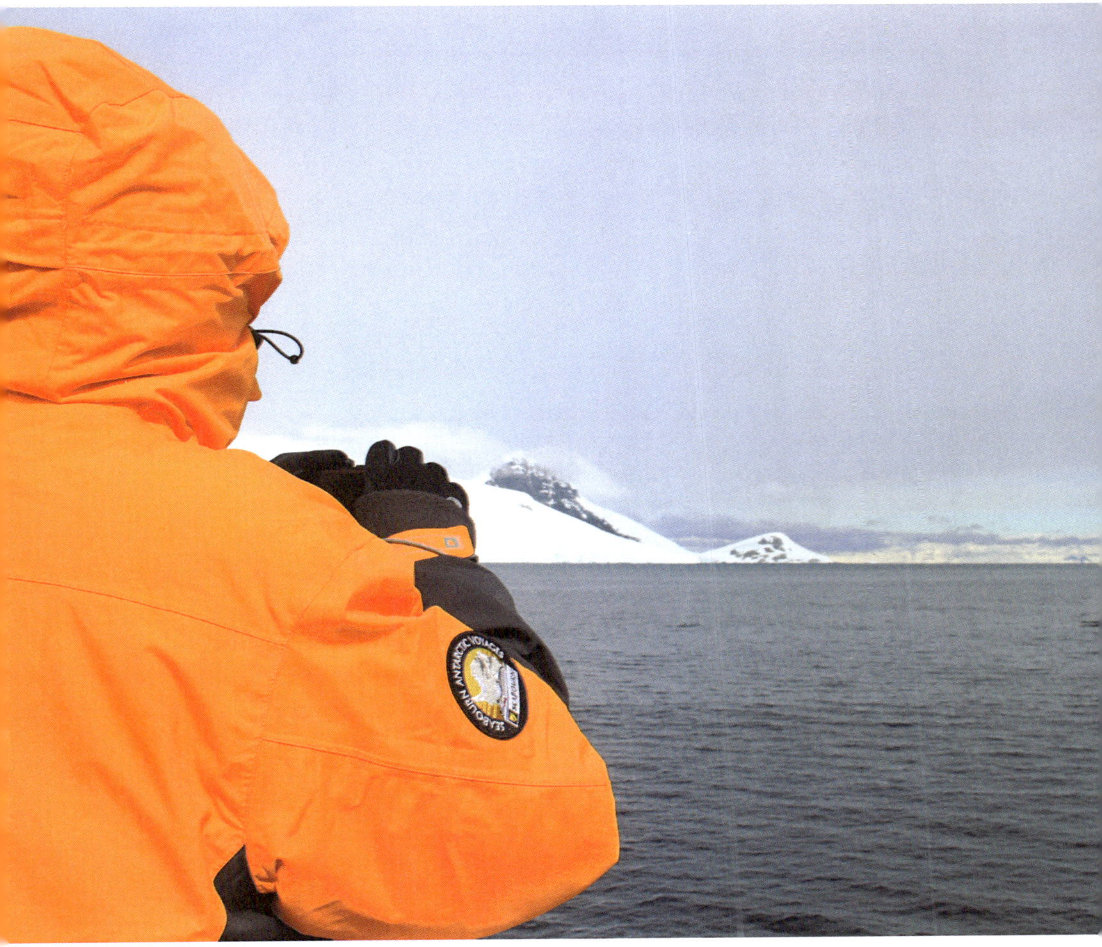

THE FINAL FRONTIER

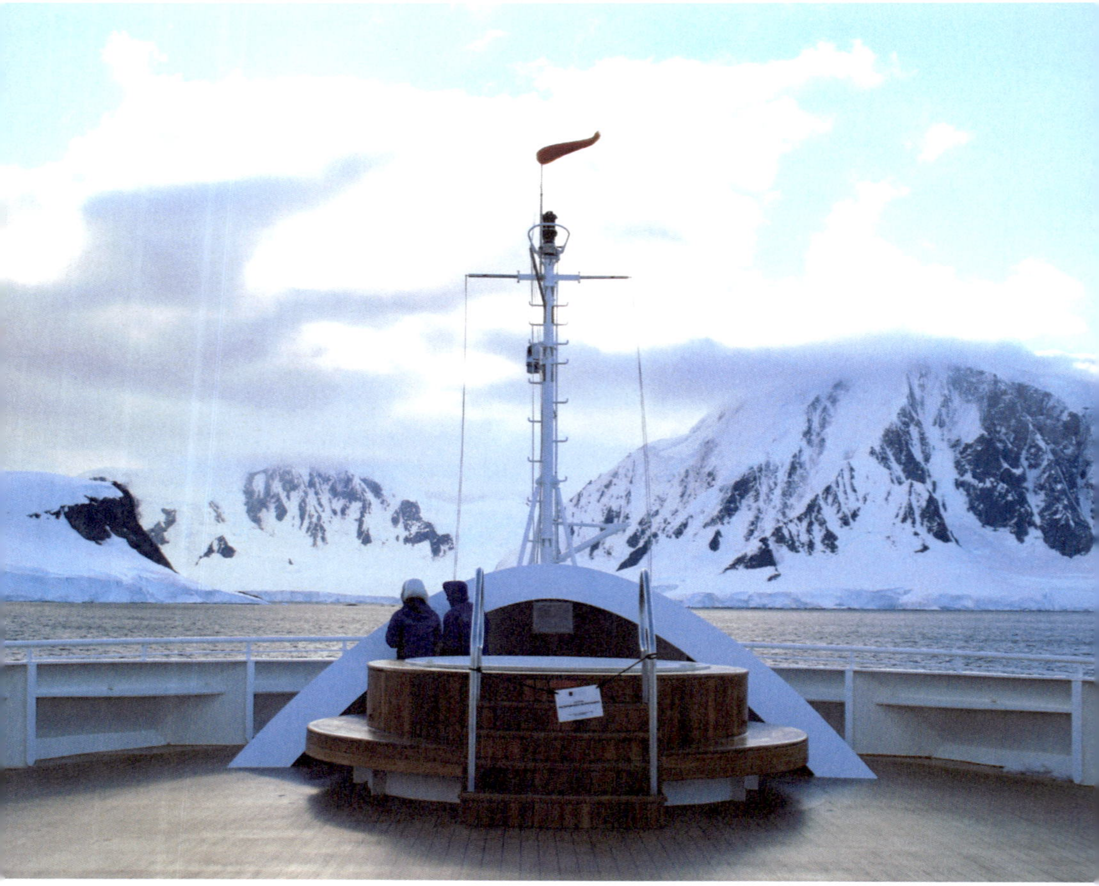

Inhabitants watchfully anticipate as a ship nears their continent.

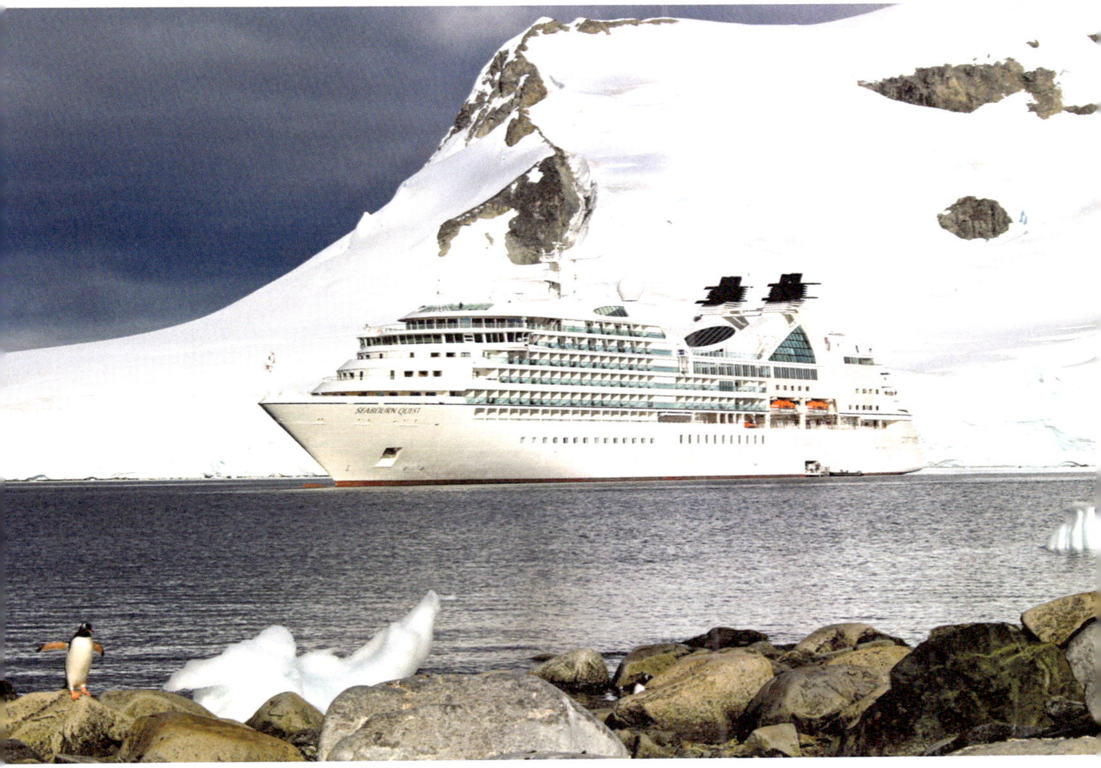

ANTARCTICA,

earth's most protected place, is an environmental preserve overseen by fifty countries for scientific research.

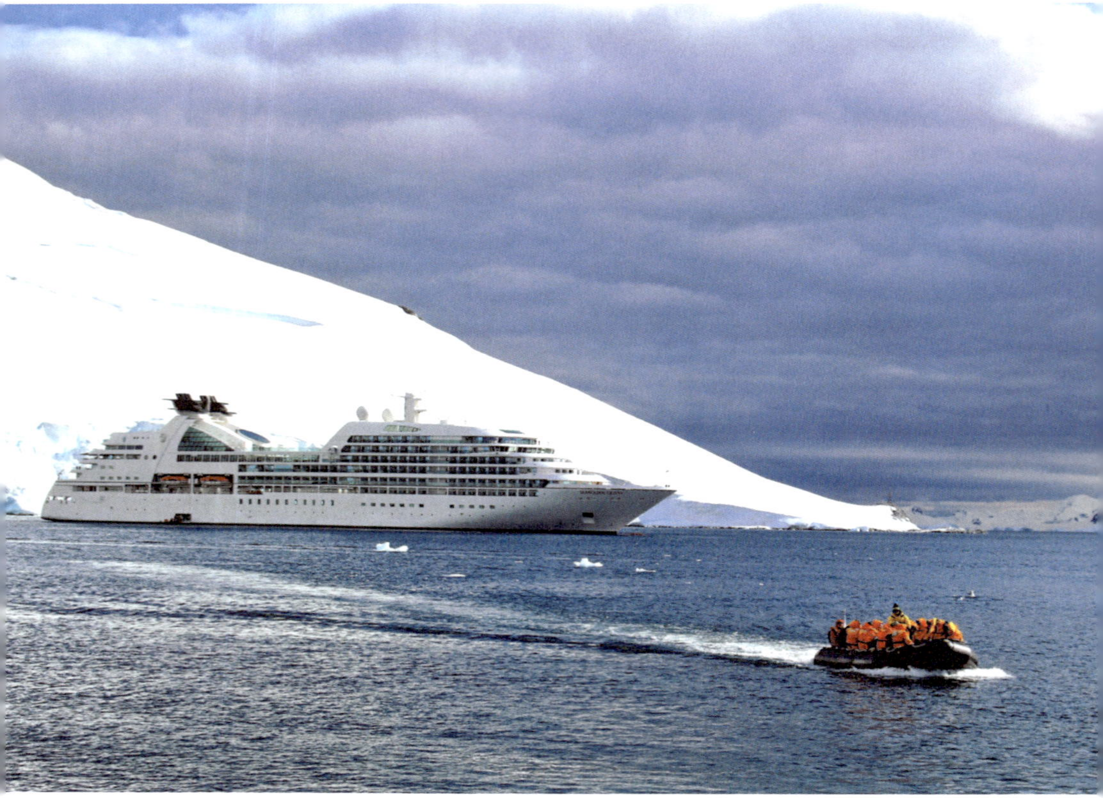

A ZODIAC,

a **small inflatable pontoon boat**, is the only method to span the distance between the ship and the ethereal land mass of ice. Only 100 people at a time may go ashore for only 90 minutes to protect this pristine wilderness.

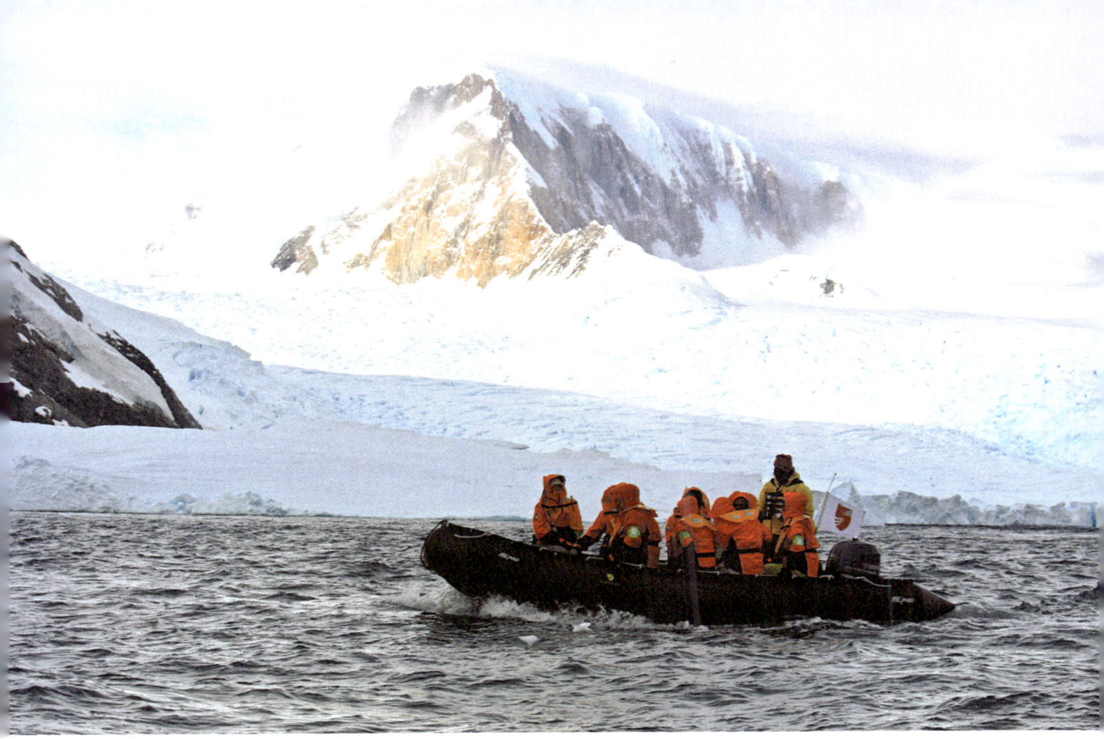

While inhaling the exhilarating Antarctic air, one quickly realizes that the ice beneath and the air above are the cleanest elements on the planet.

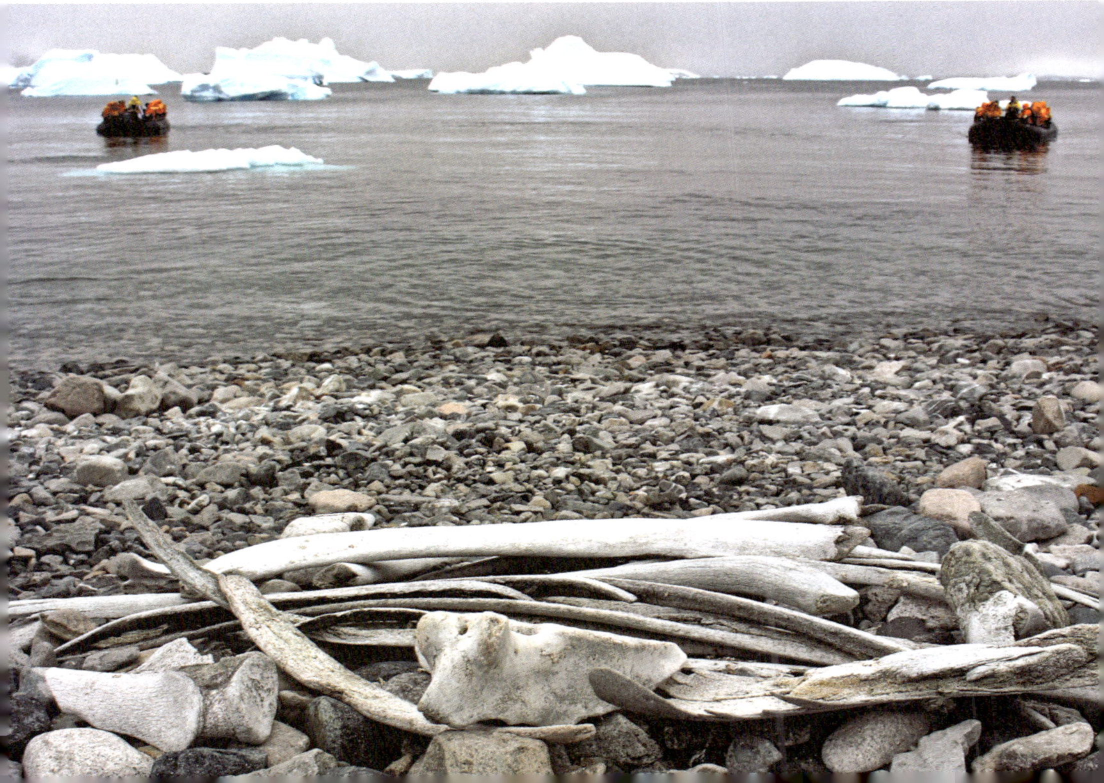

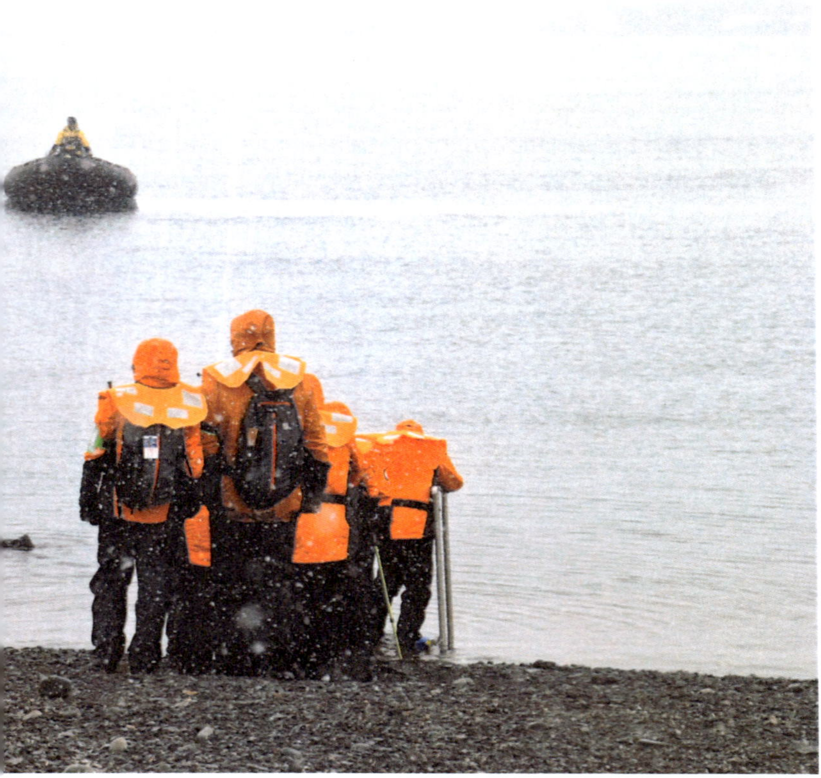

Before going ashore, every visitor must step into a disinfectant bath for boots; no loose paper or plastic can be taken on shore; *no smoking is allowed.*

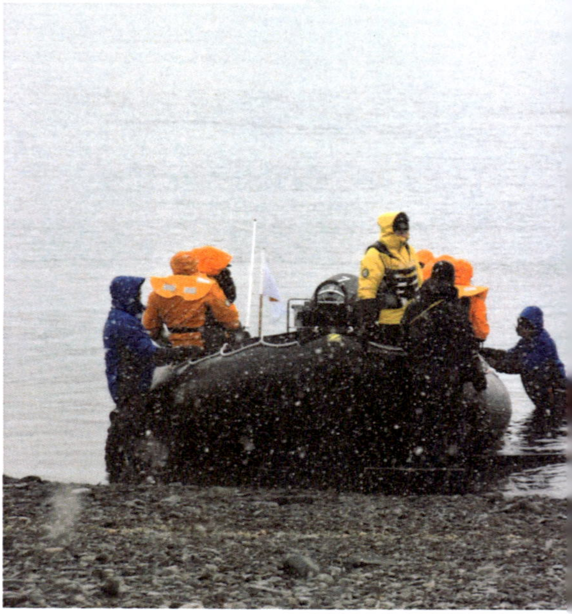

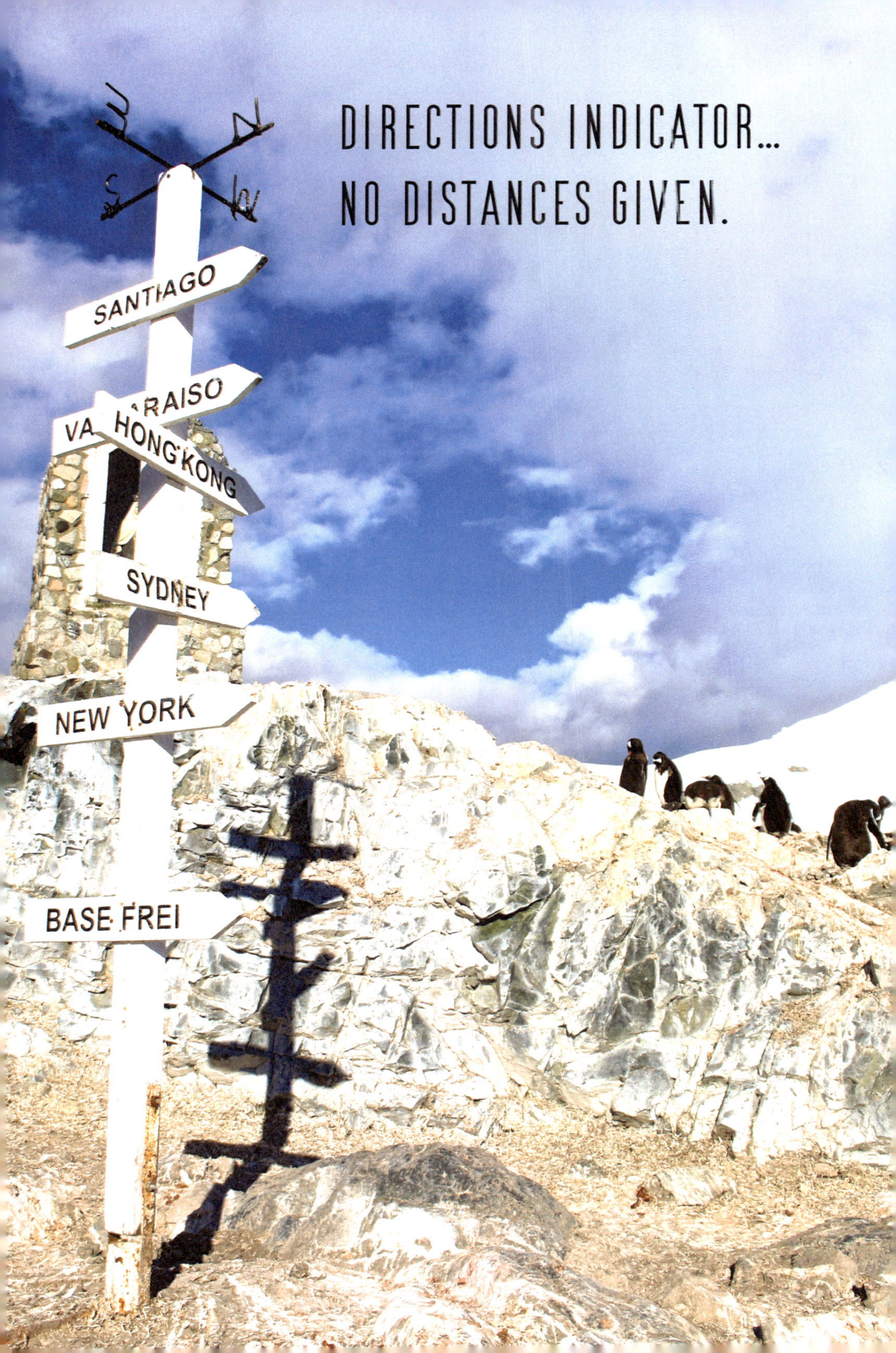

DIRECTIONS INDICATOR...
NO DISTANCES GIVEN.

Upon arrival, a first observation is that of the coexistence of species, as a walrus lazily basks in the morning sun while busy penguins jump in and out of the water gathering their breakfasts.

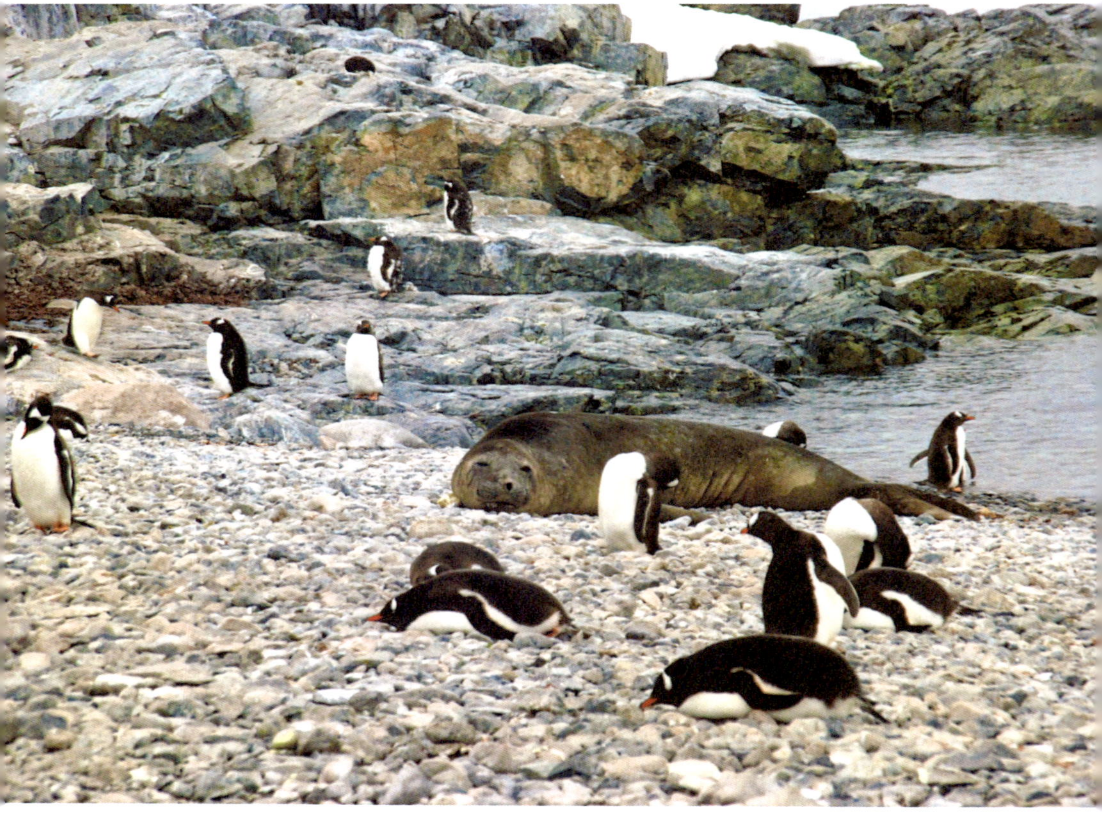

THE EUPHORIC MOMENT...

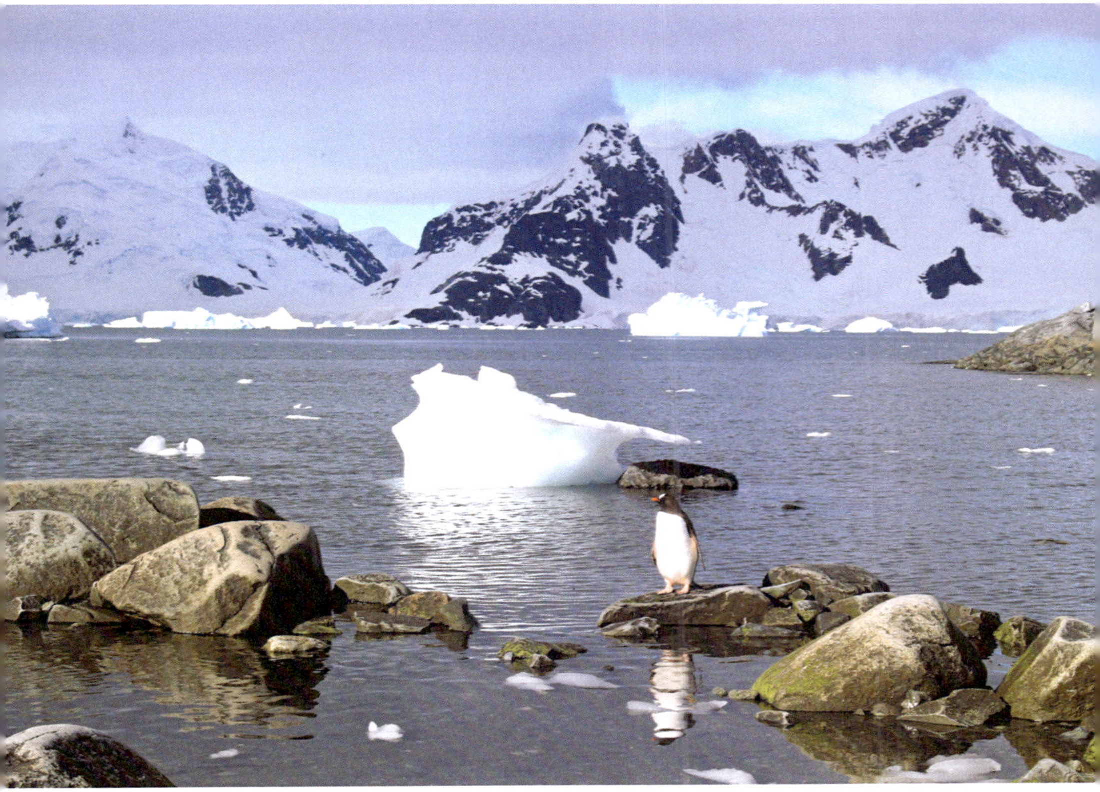

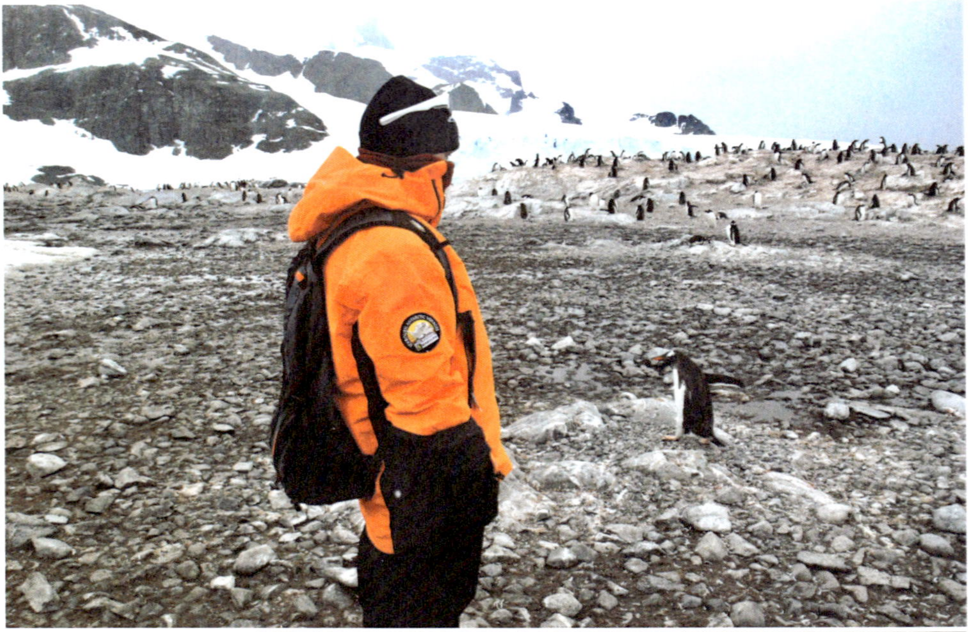

... can be quickly interrupted as tuxedoed inhabitants waddle by to check out the visitors.

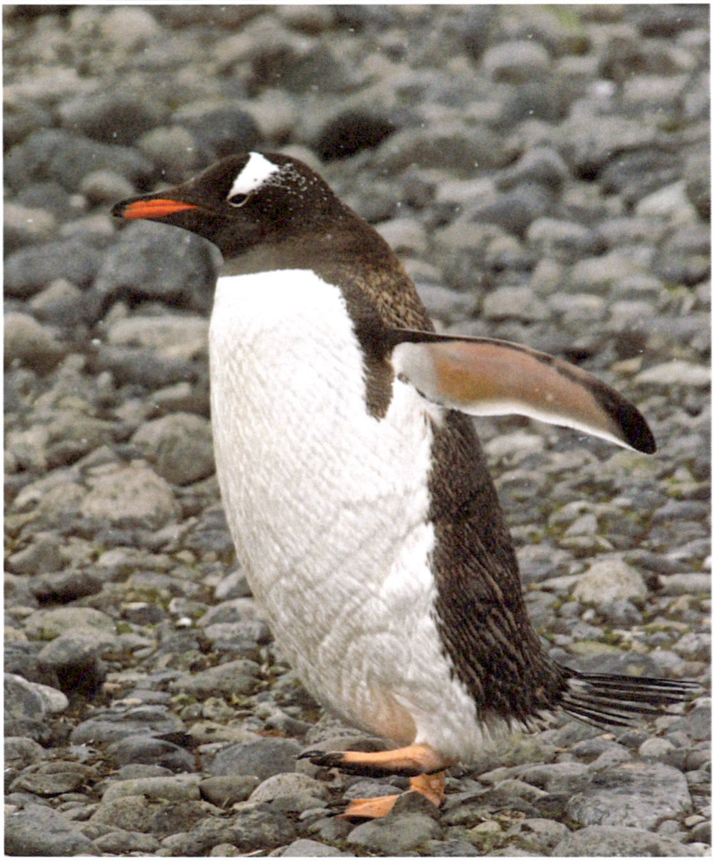

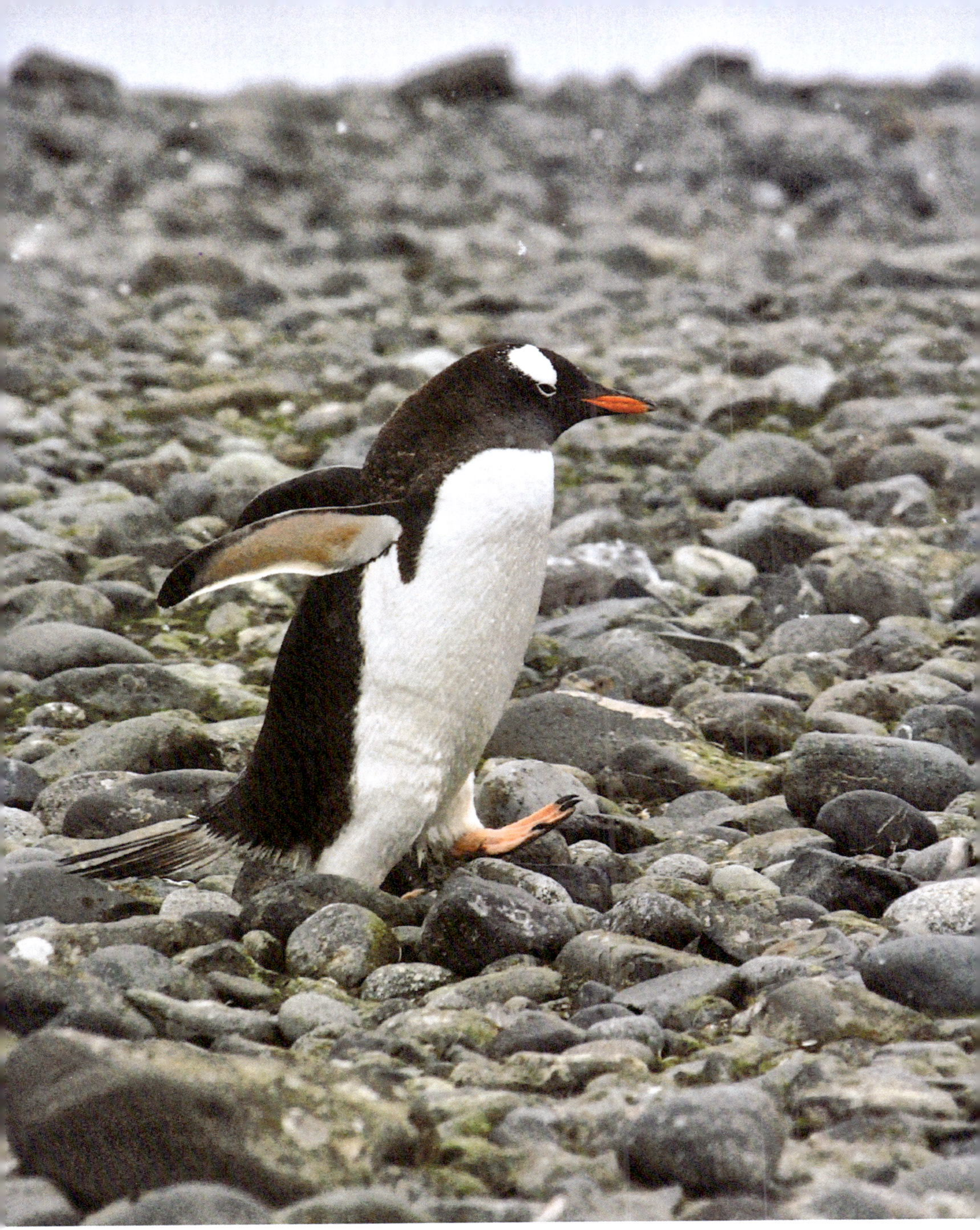

They may scurry off, with flippers held wide, for balance, or...

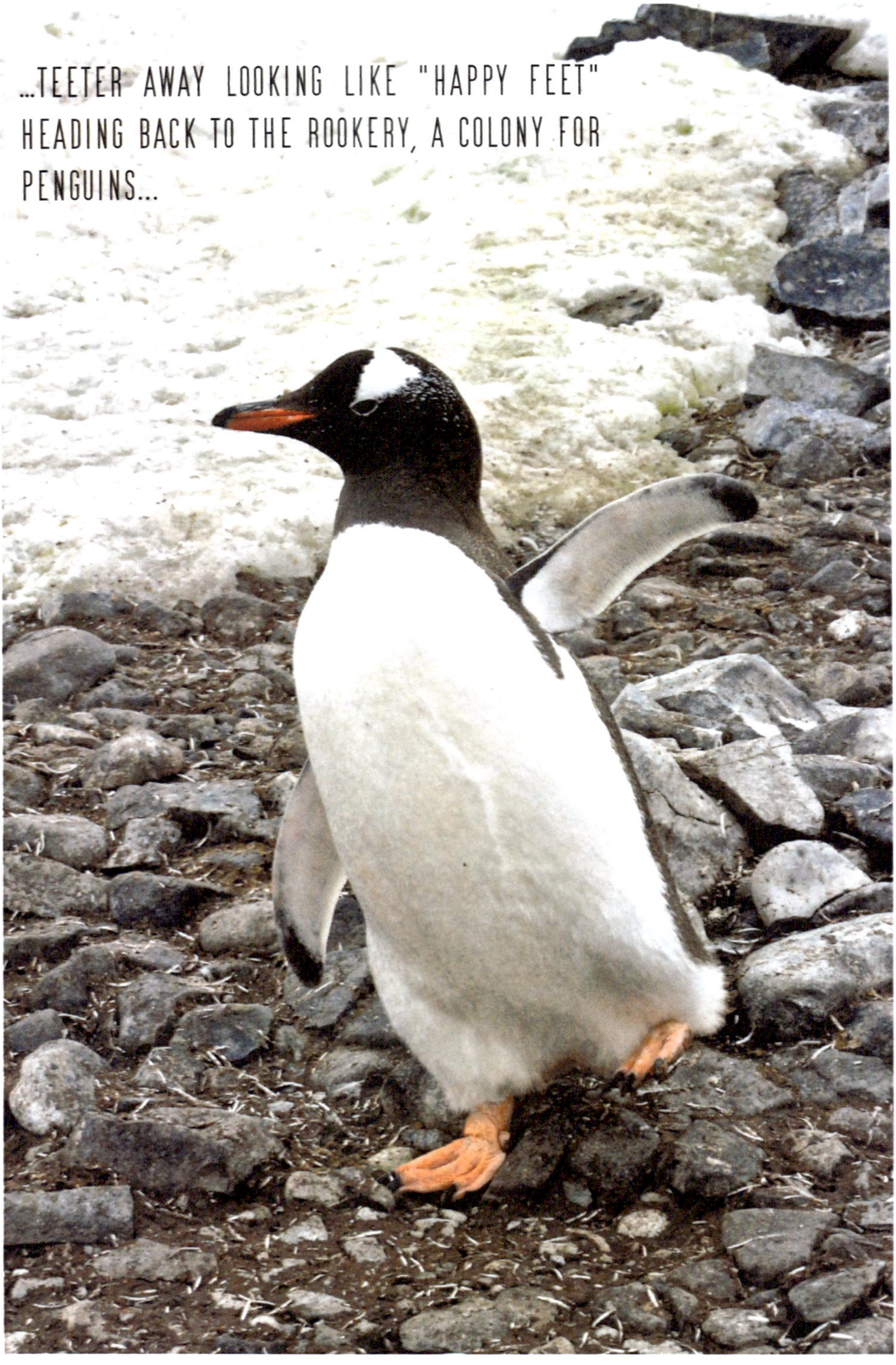
...TEETER AWAY LOOKING LIKE "HAPPY FEET" HEADING BACK TO THE ROOKERY, A COLONY FOR PENGUINS...

some are diving into the sea ...

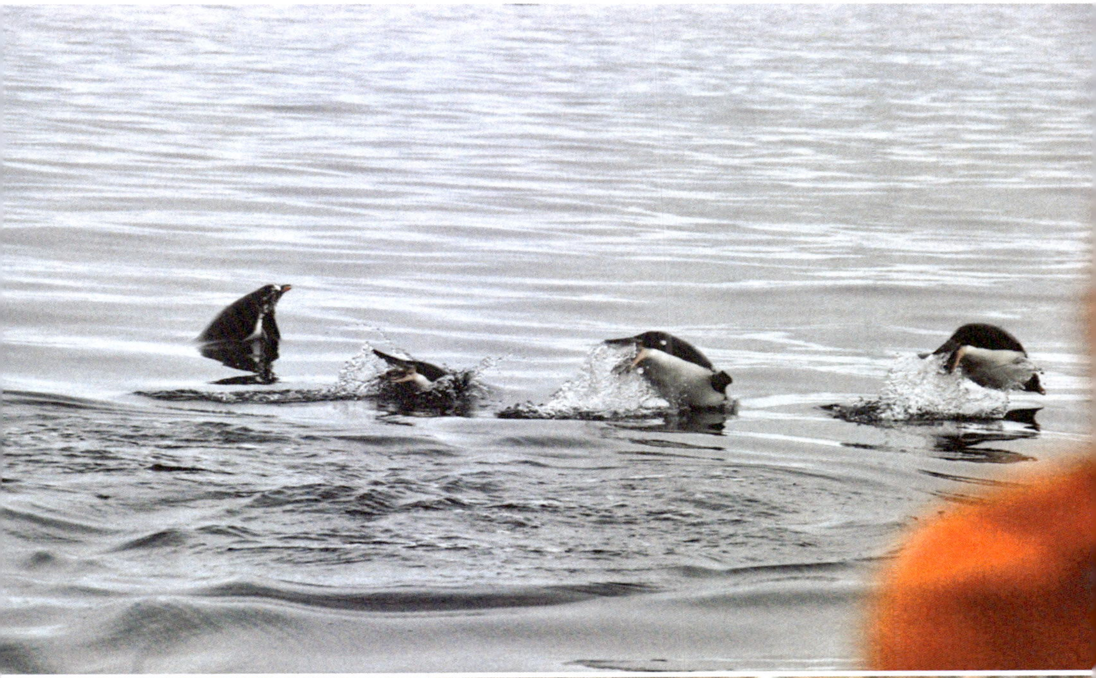

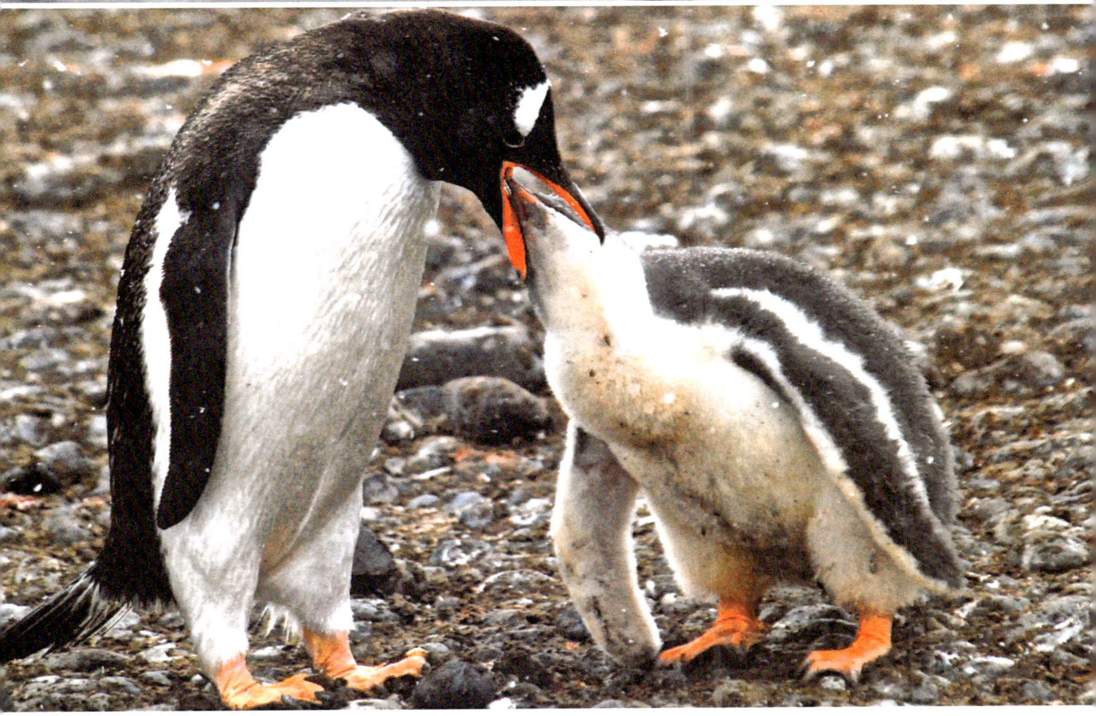

... while others return to feed their young.

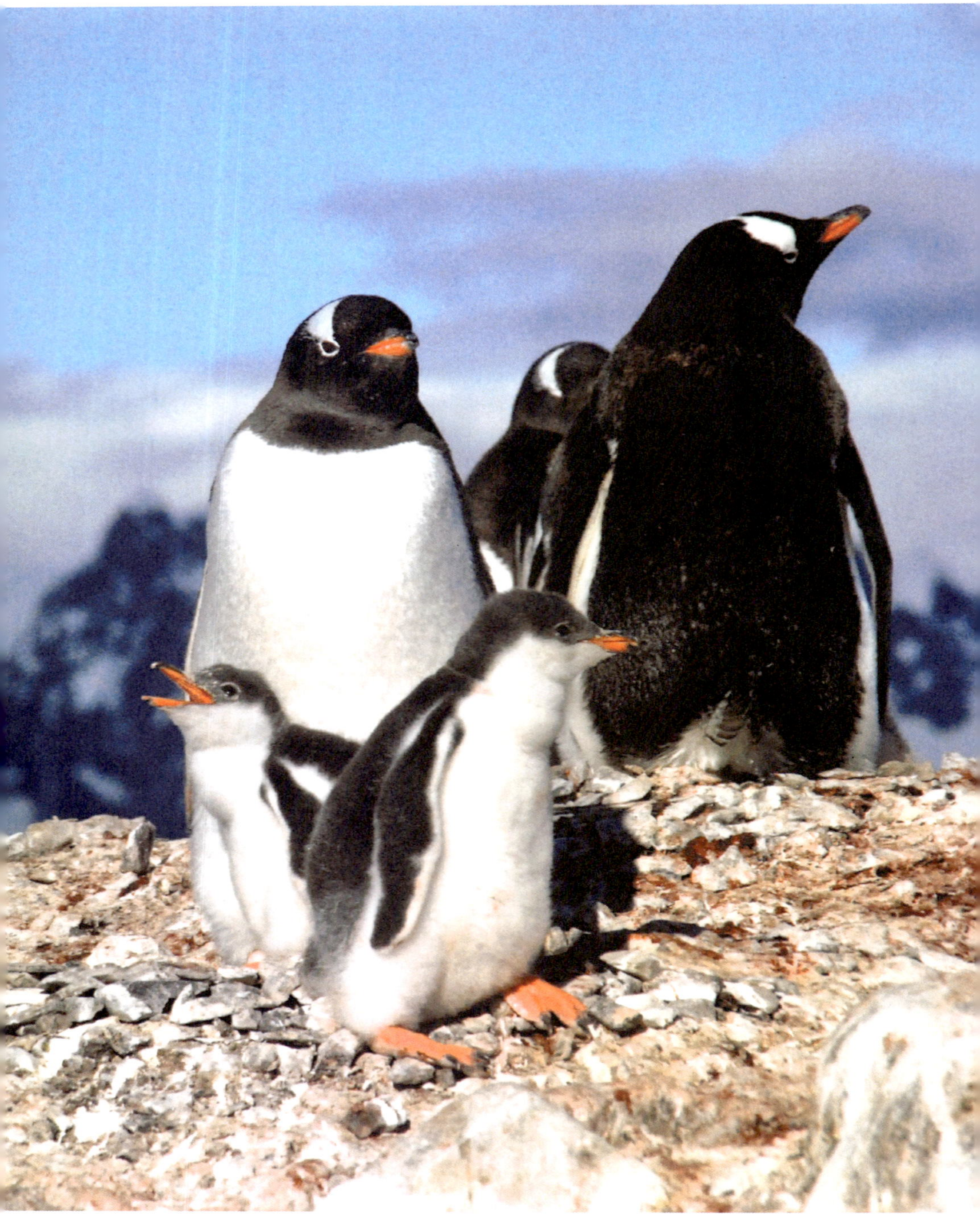

Some are keeping a watchful eye ...

... for predatory birds threatening their colony.

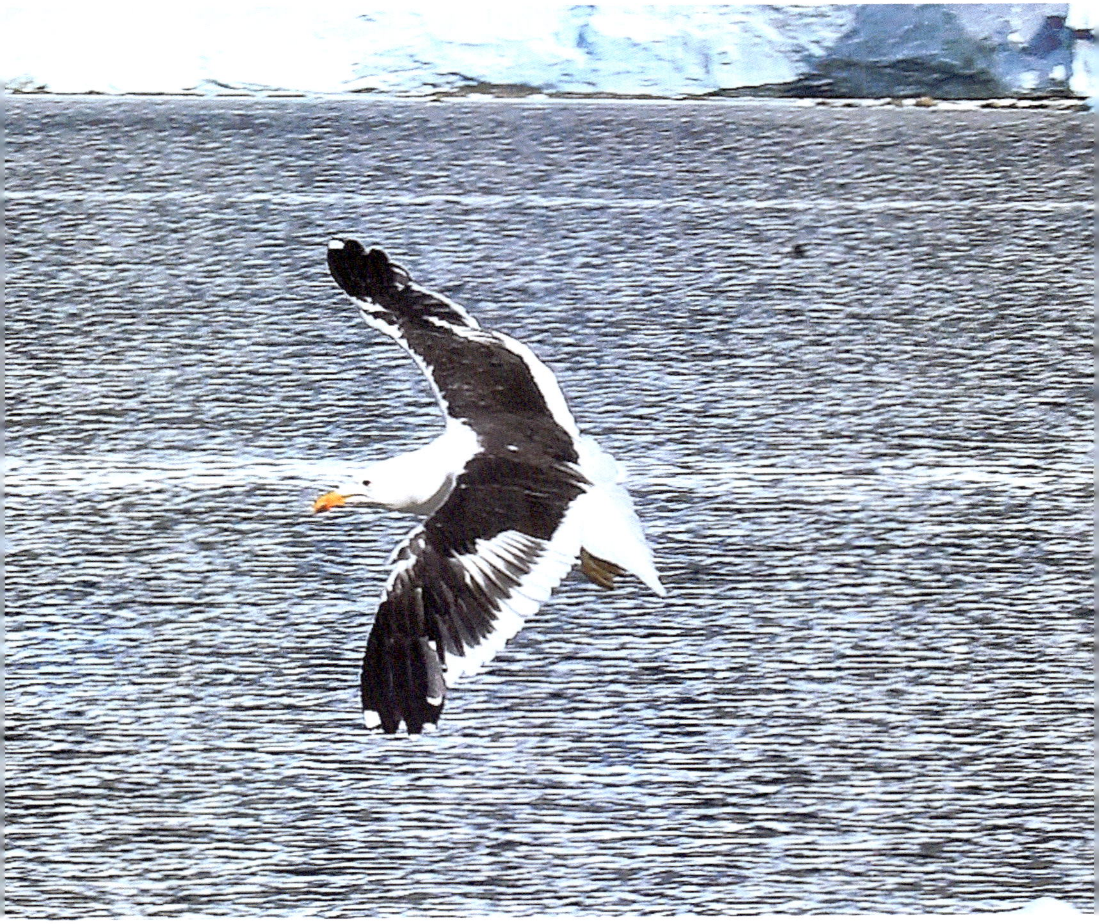

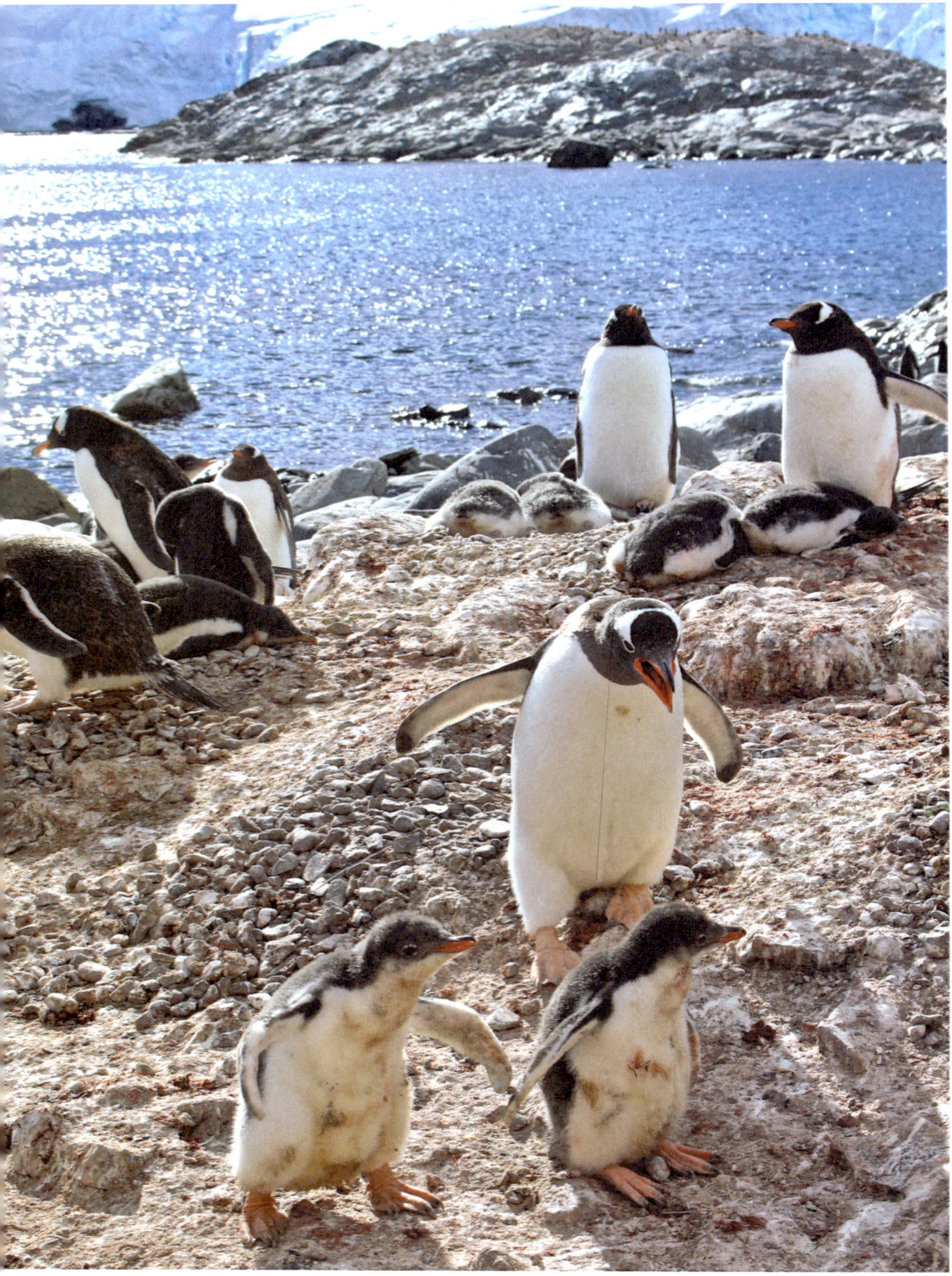

Some are scolding their young...

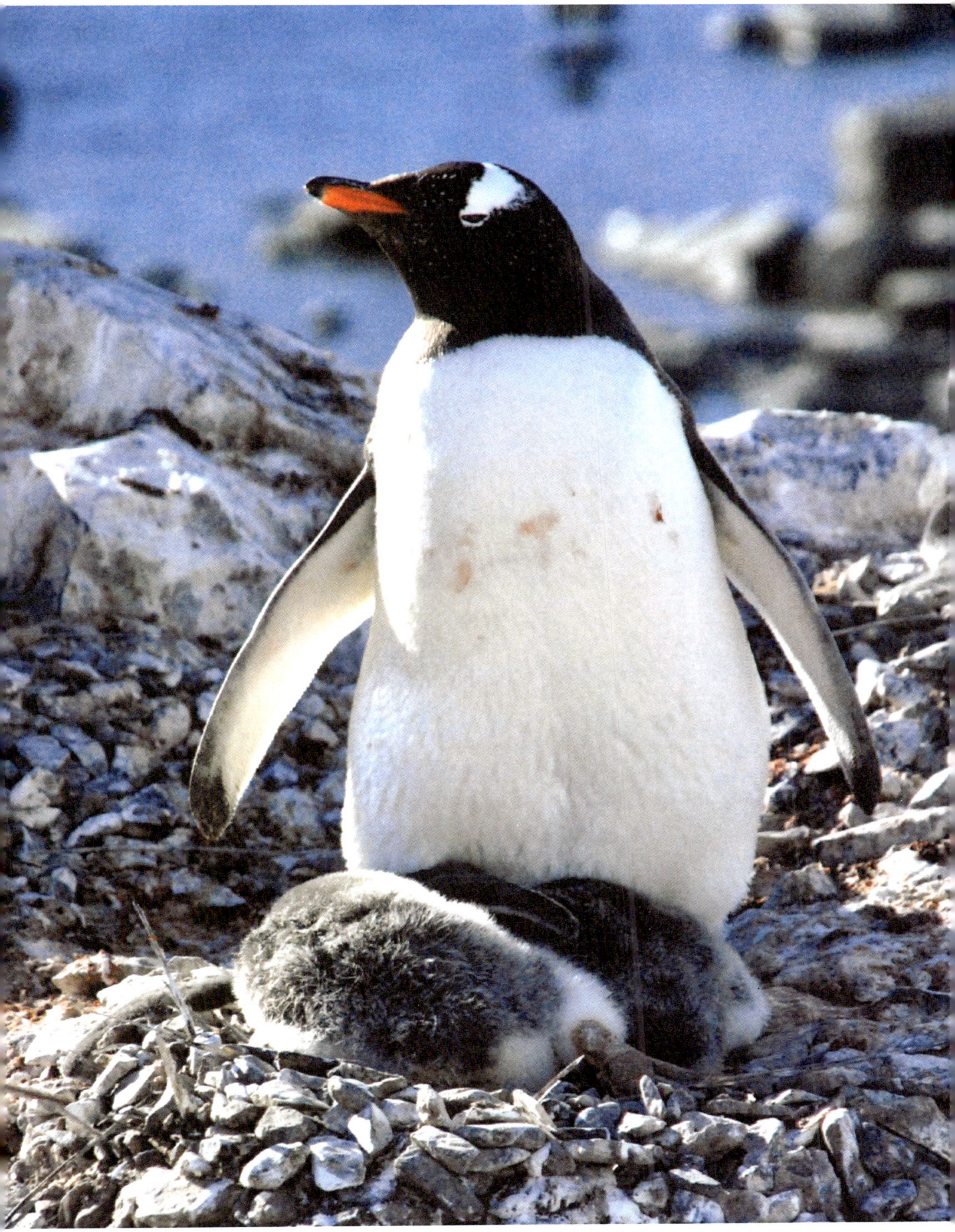

...while others remain with their sleeping chicks.

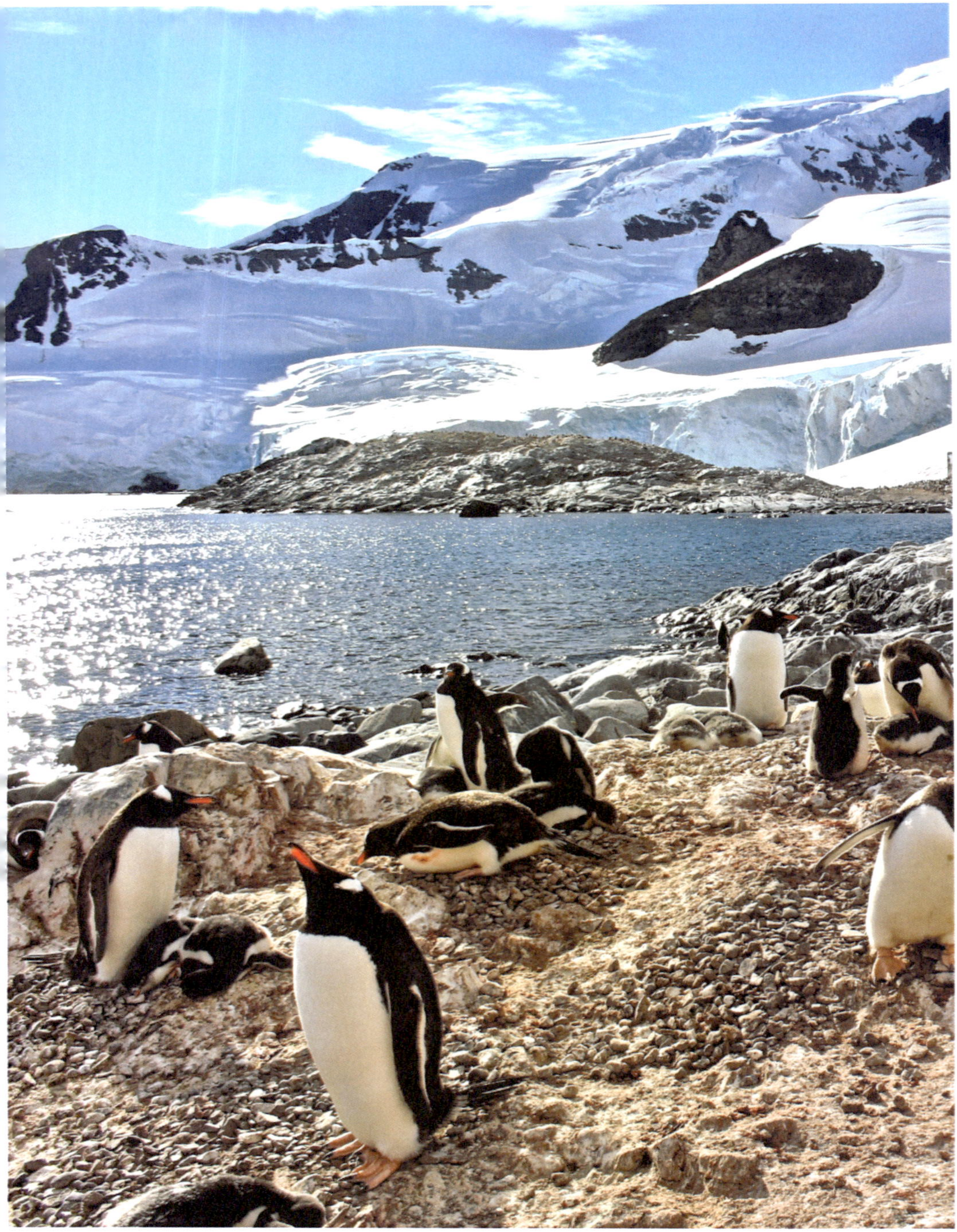

Many enjoy the extended colony families...

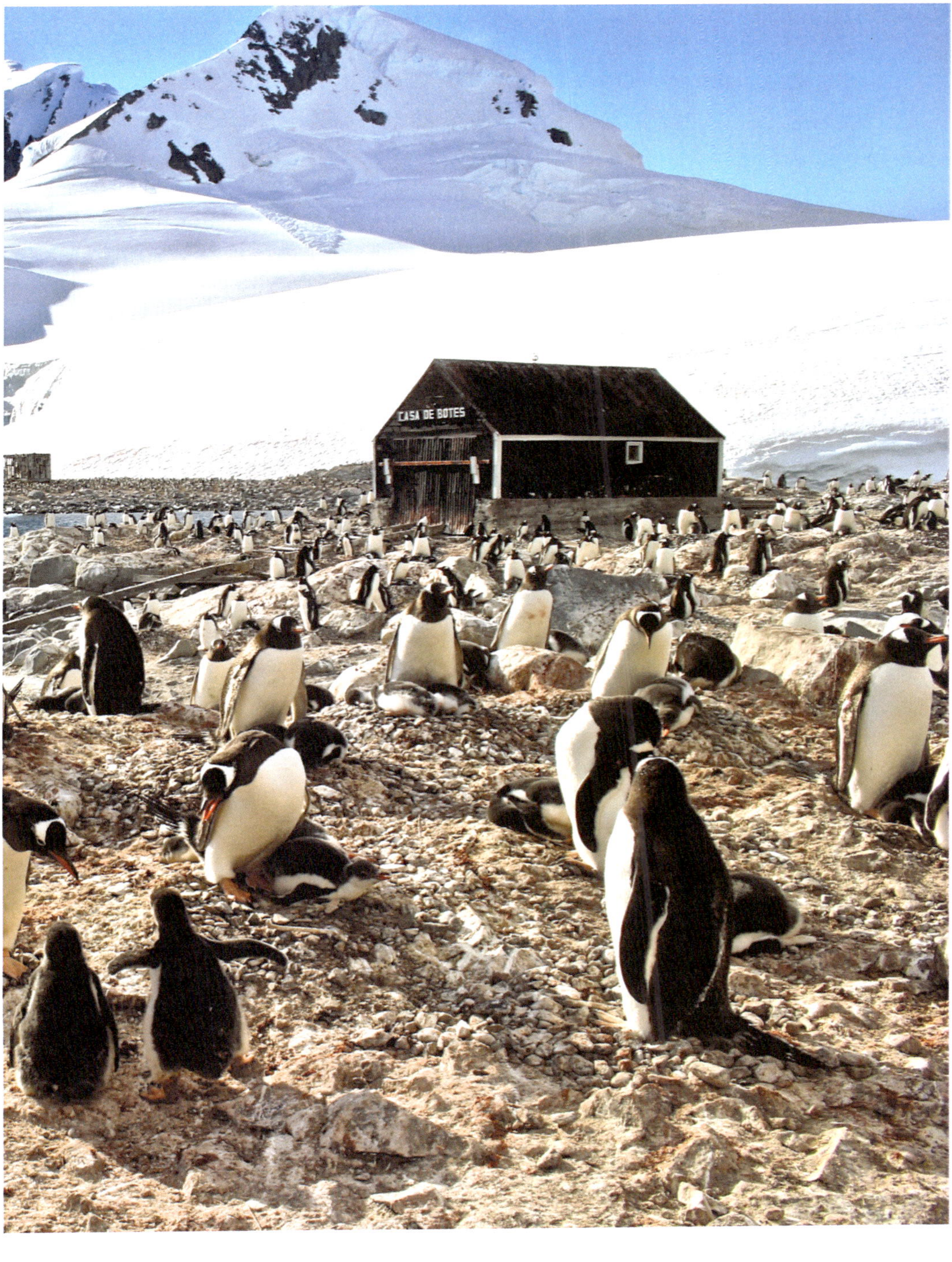
CASA DE BOTES

...while some solitary individuals venture somberly alone.

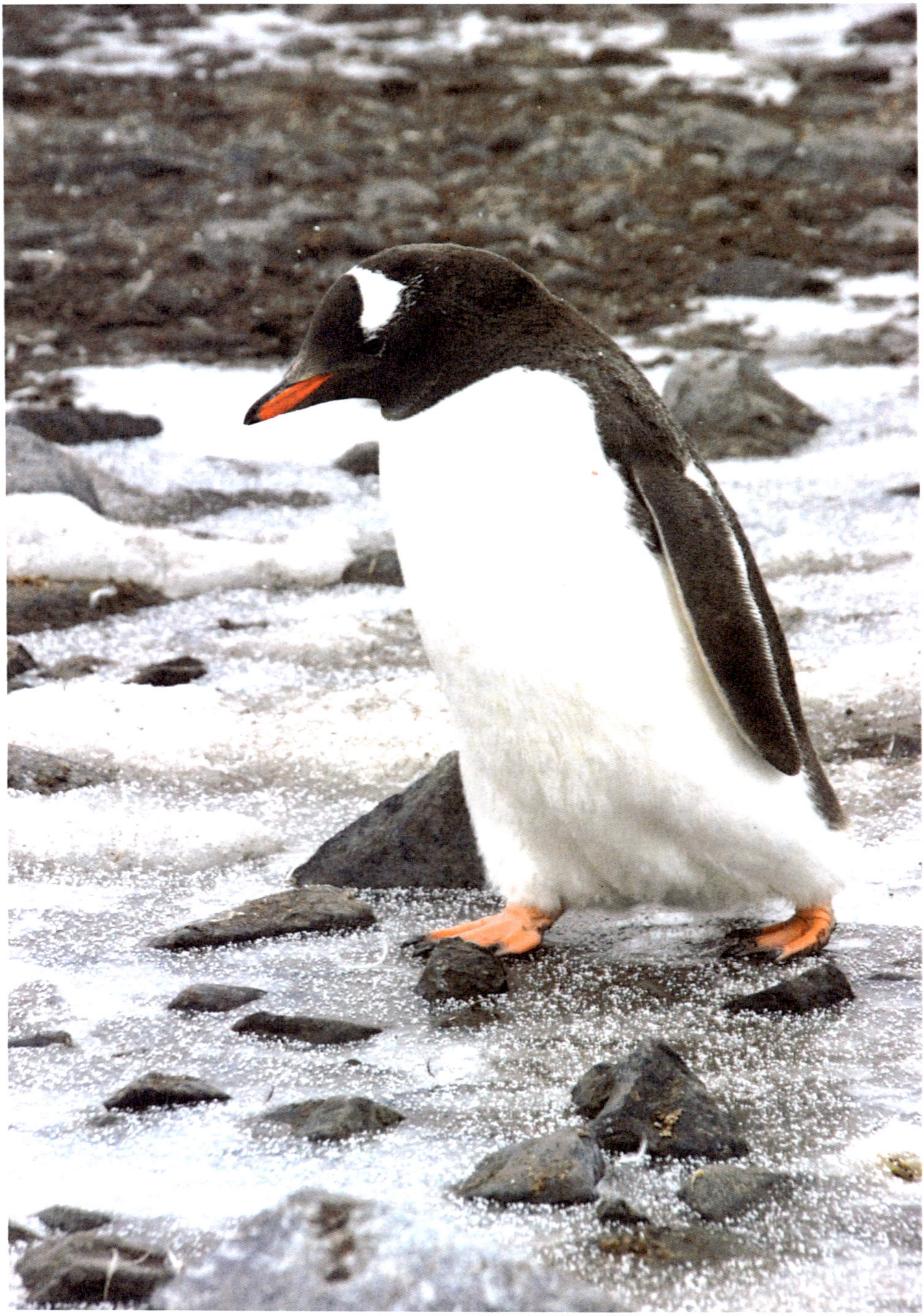

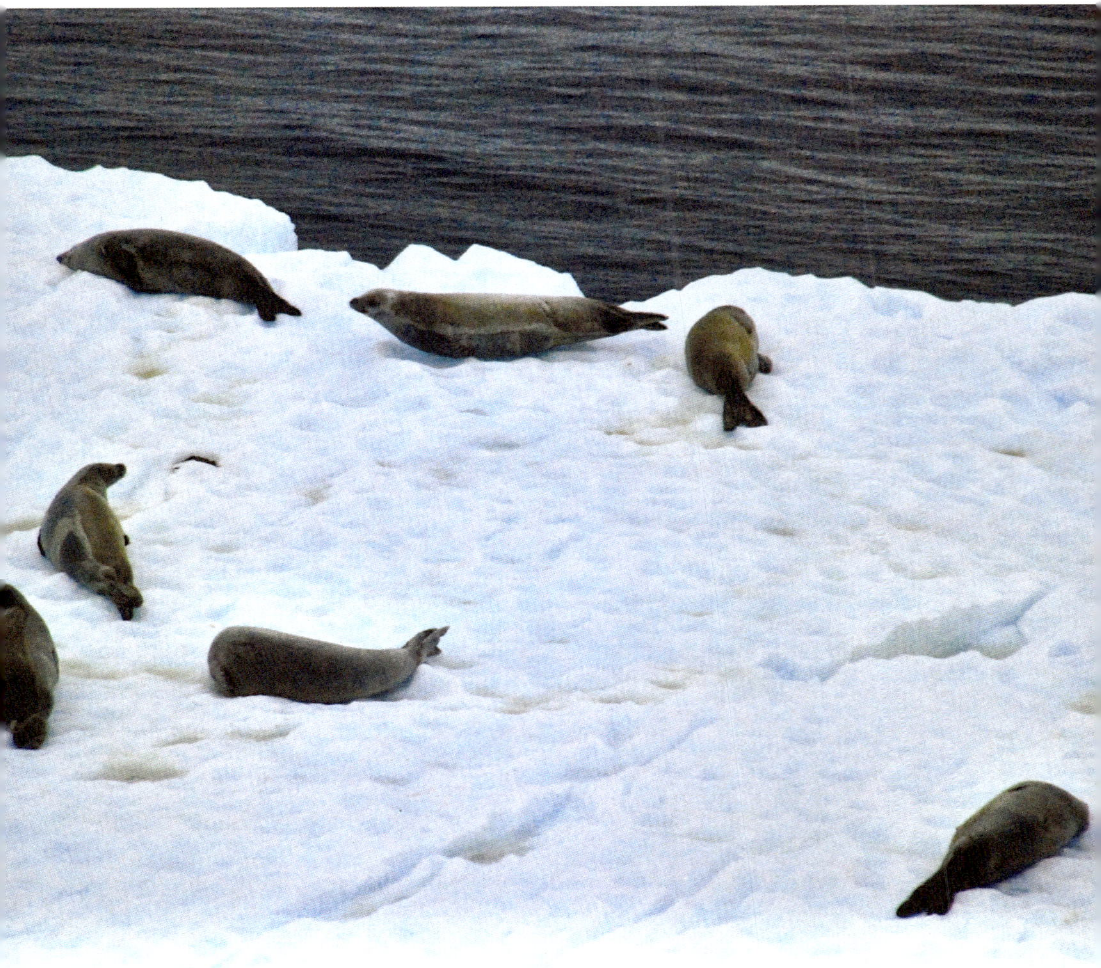

WILDLIFE

is abundant in this southern-most world. Small ice floes, dotted with families of seals rest between dives.

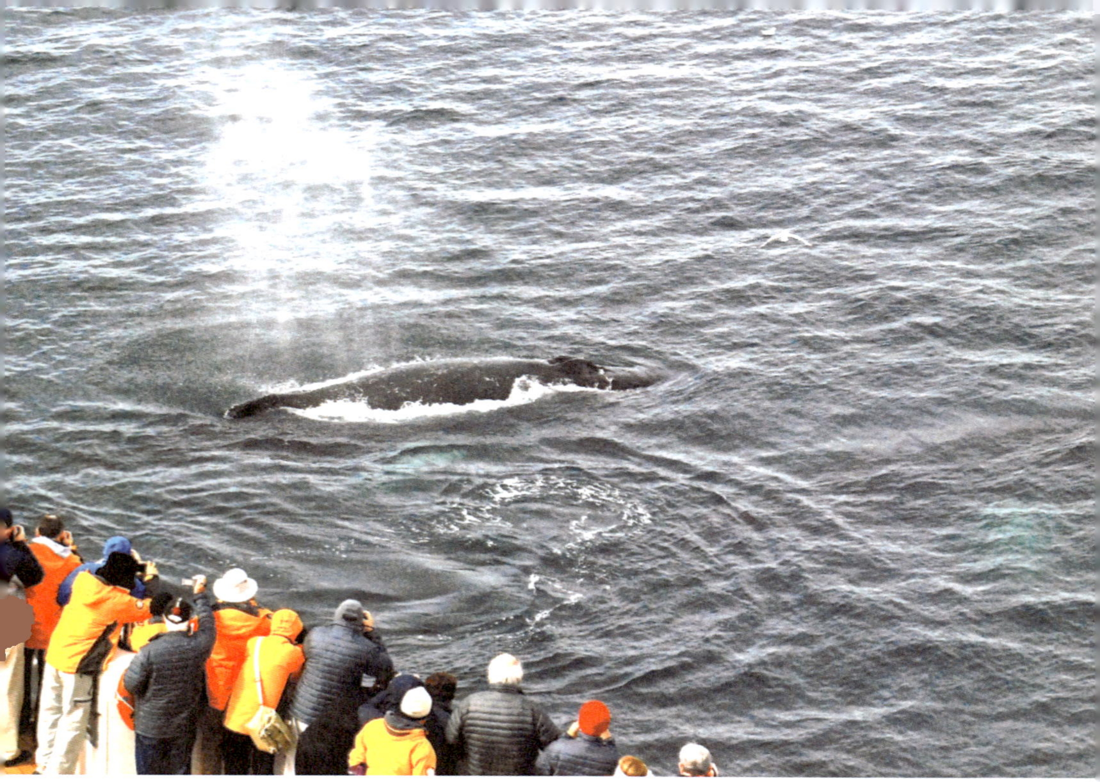

WHALES DANCE FROM ONE SIDE OF THE SHIP TO THE OTHER.

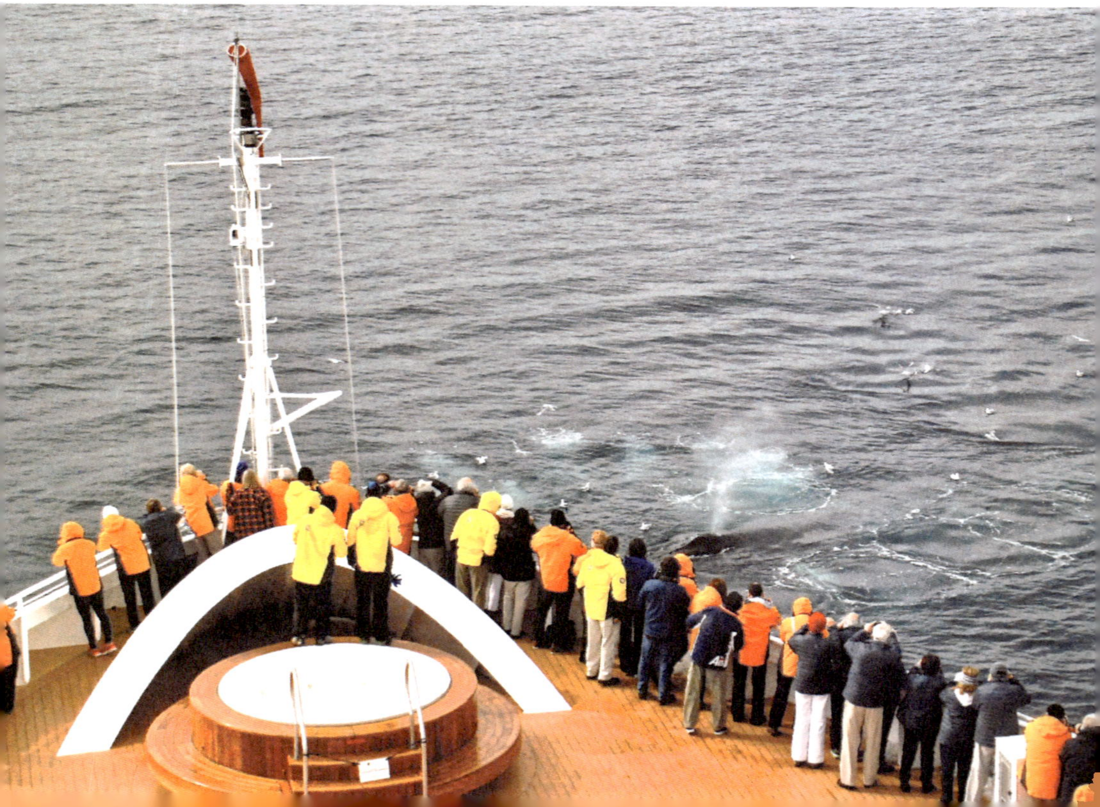

Bubble net feeding is a sophisticated, cooperative feeding method. While the whales communicate by vocalizations, the small fish schools become disoriented and corralled into a "net" of bubbles.

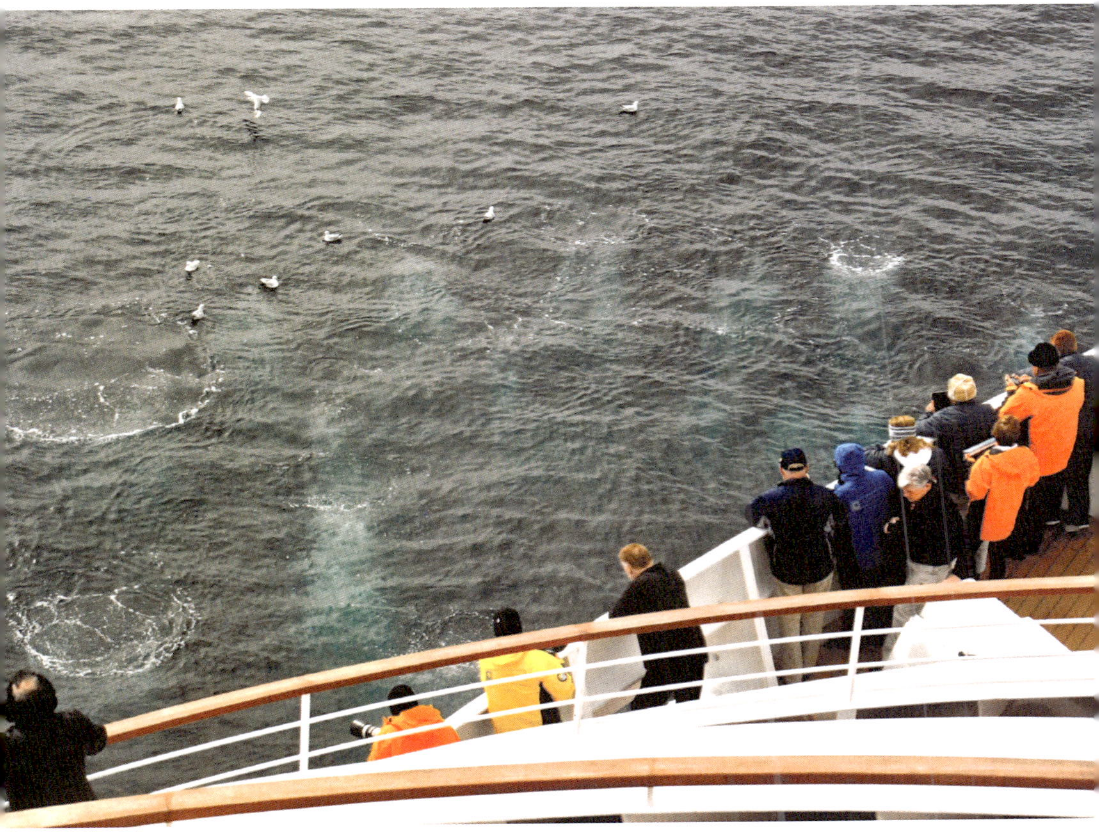

These deep sea kings swim upward like synchronized swimmers, mouths wide open to feed on the trapped fish… an amazing moment in nature.

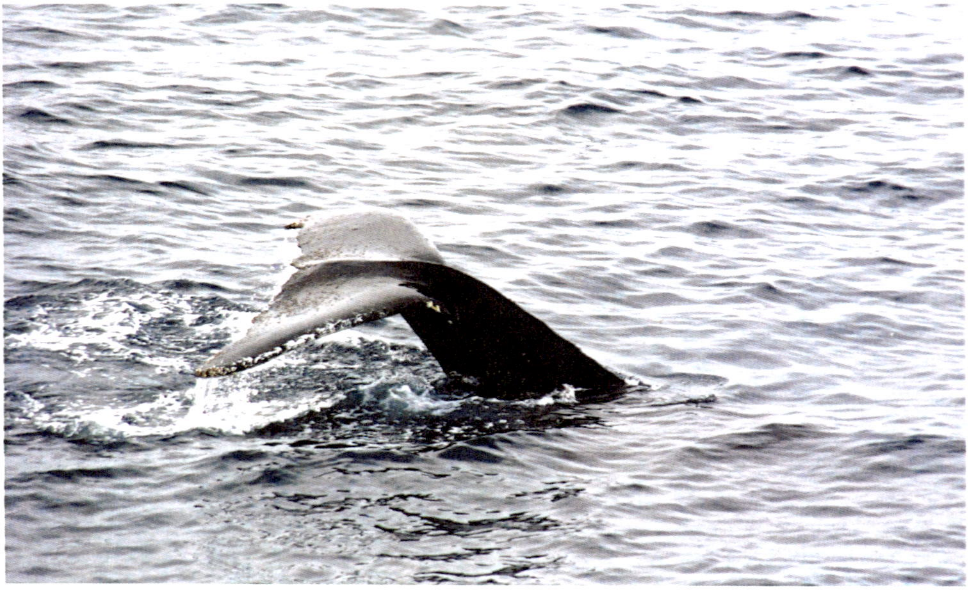

LOOKING LIKE A SUBMARINE ...

AND DIVING.

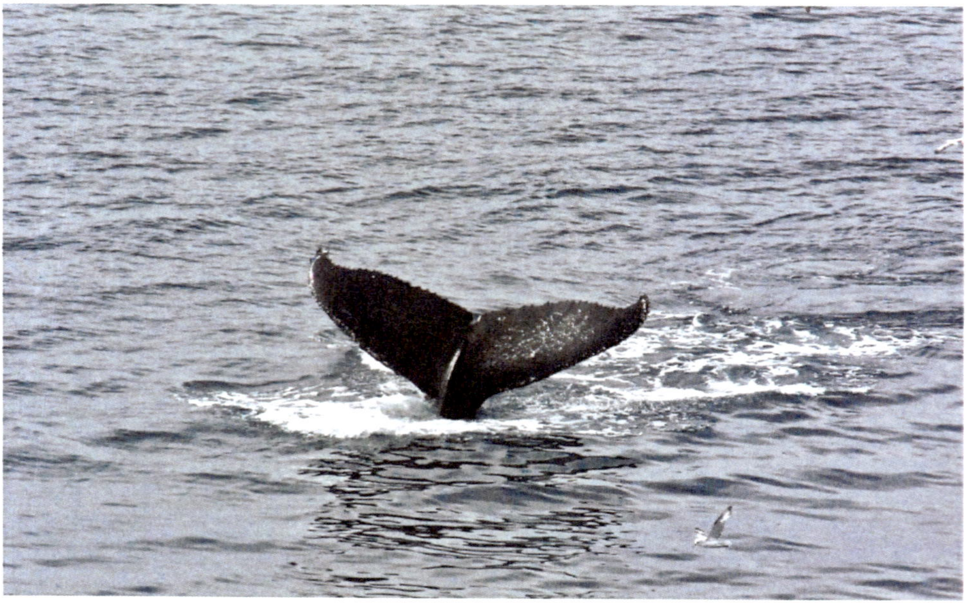

Watching the tails of these mammoth sea creatures as they silently swim away is enhanced by the pristine white sculptured background that is a cherished, unforgettable display of the marvel of

ANTARCTICA

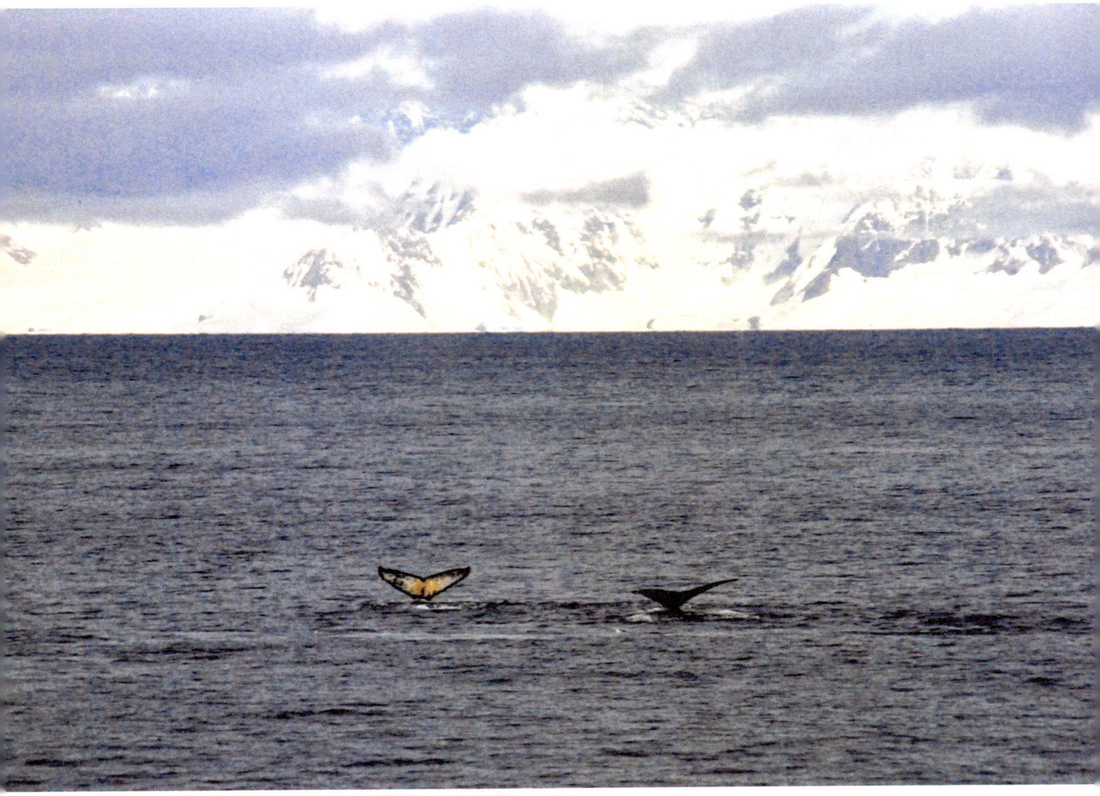

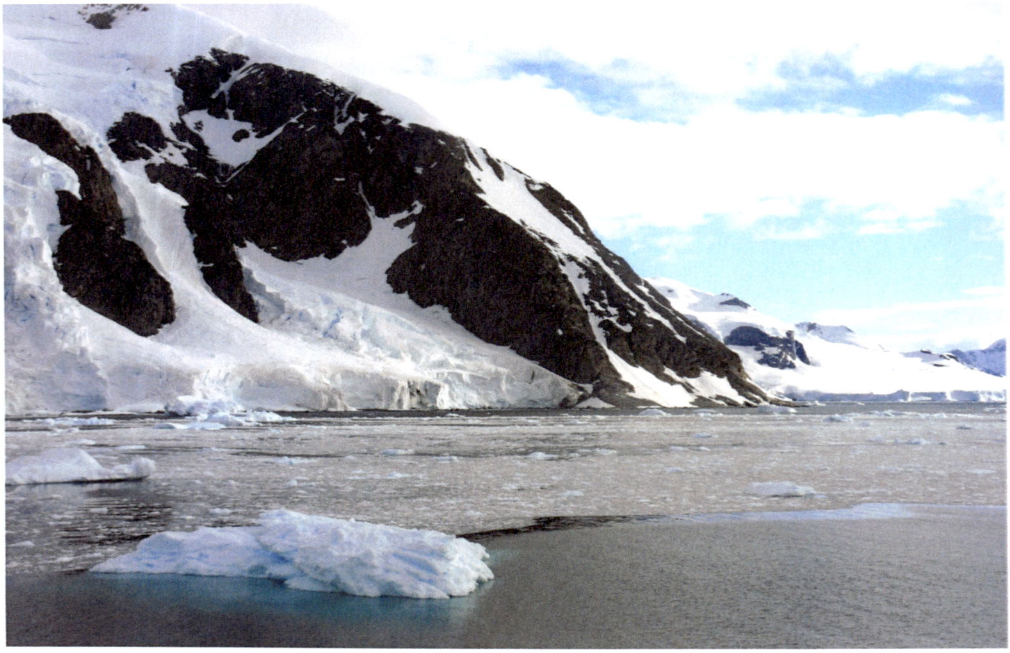

When the Antarctic fresh glacial water meets the salty ocean water, a definite line forms as the less dense fresh water rises to the top.

ANTARCTICA is NOT solid white!

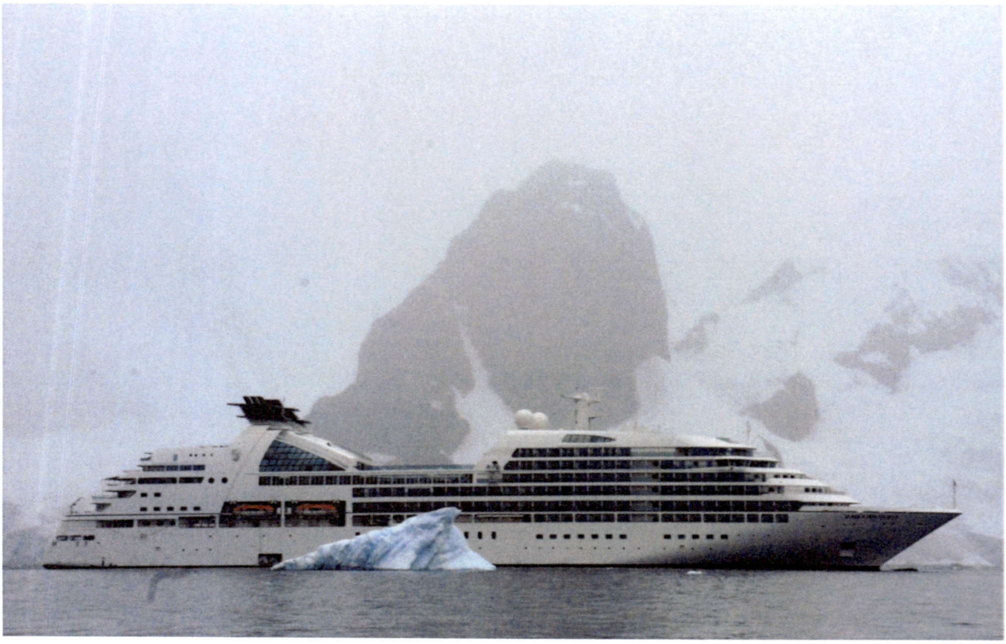

Due to the ice density, blue ice formations frequently appear...

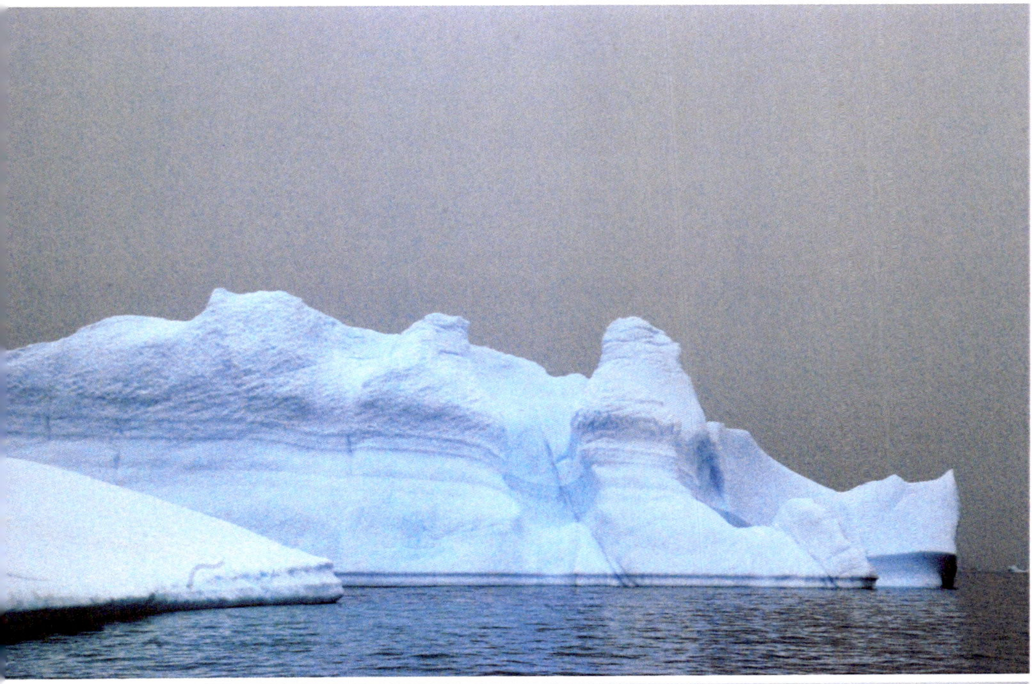

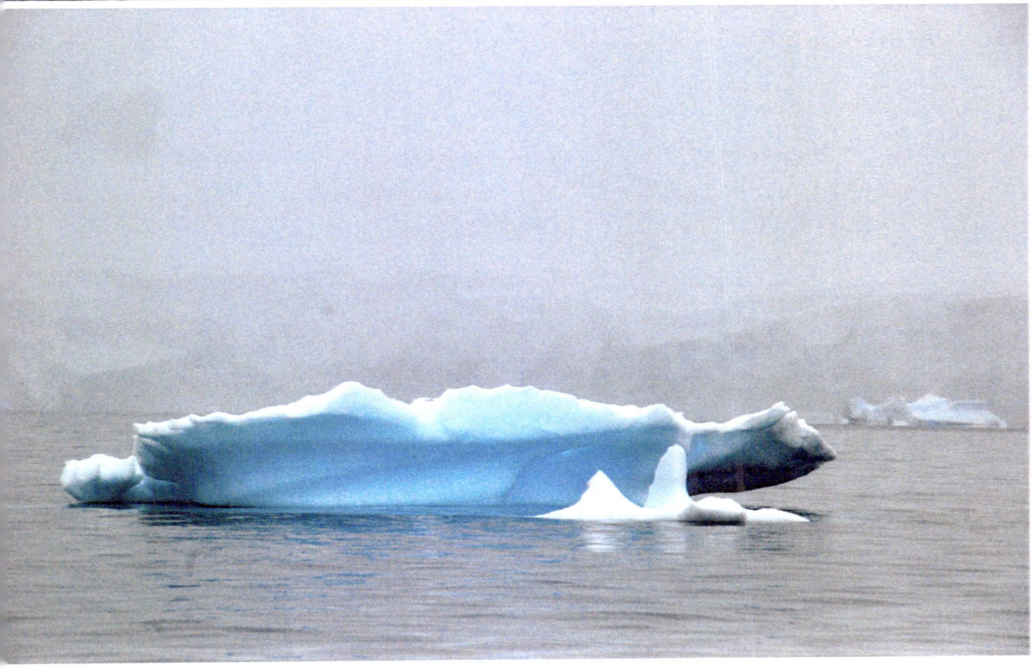

...such as this turtle shaped iceberg...

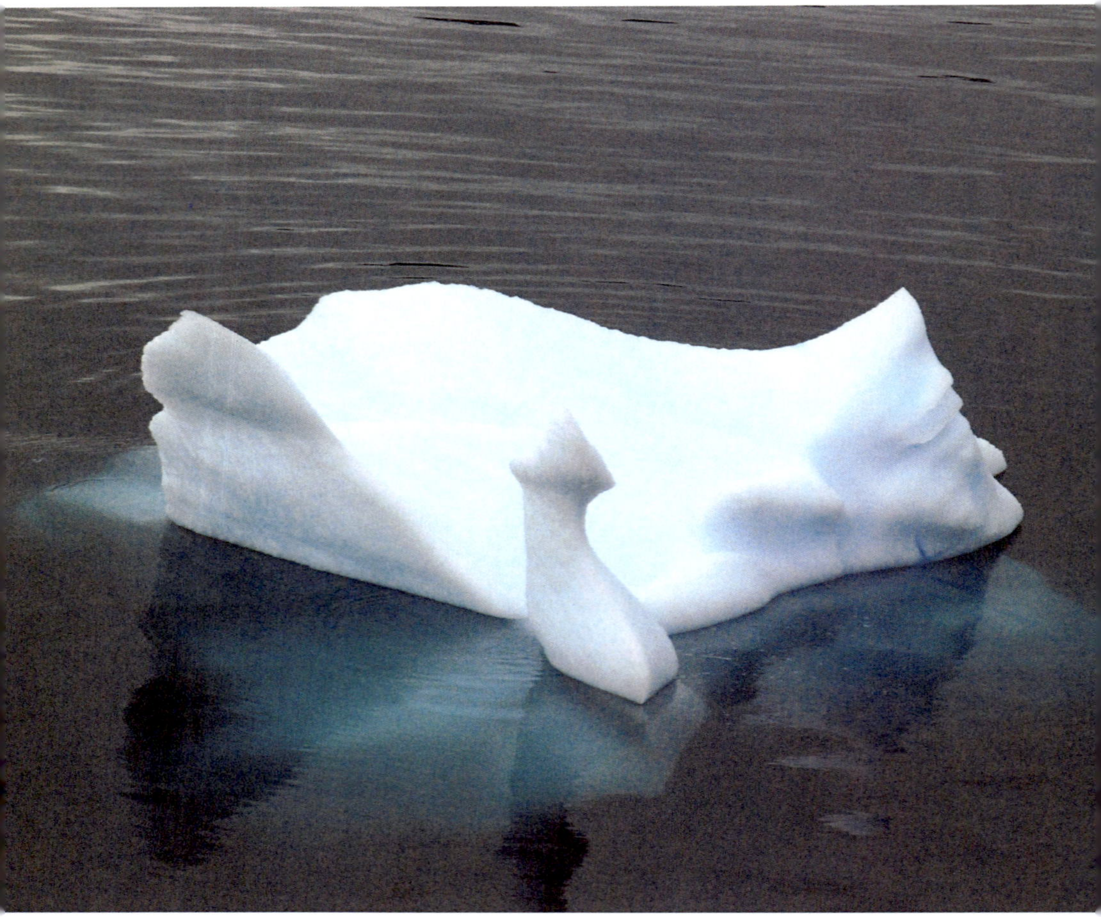

... or this BLUE"SWAN"
exhibiting its half-spread wings.

EXPLORERS must prepare each day for the unpredictable...

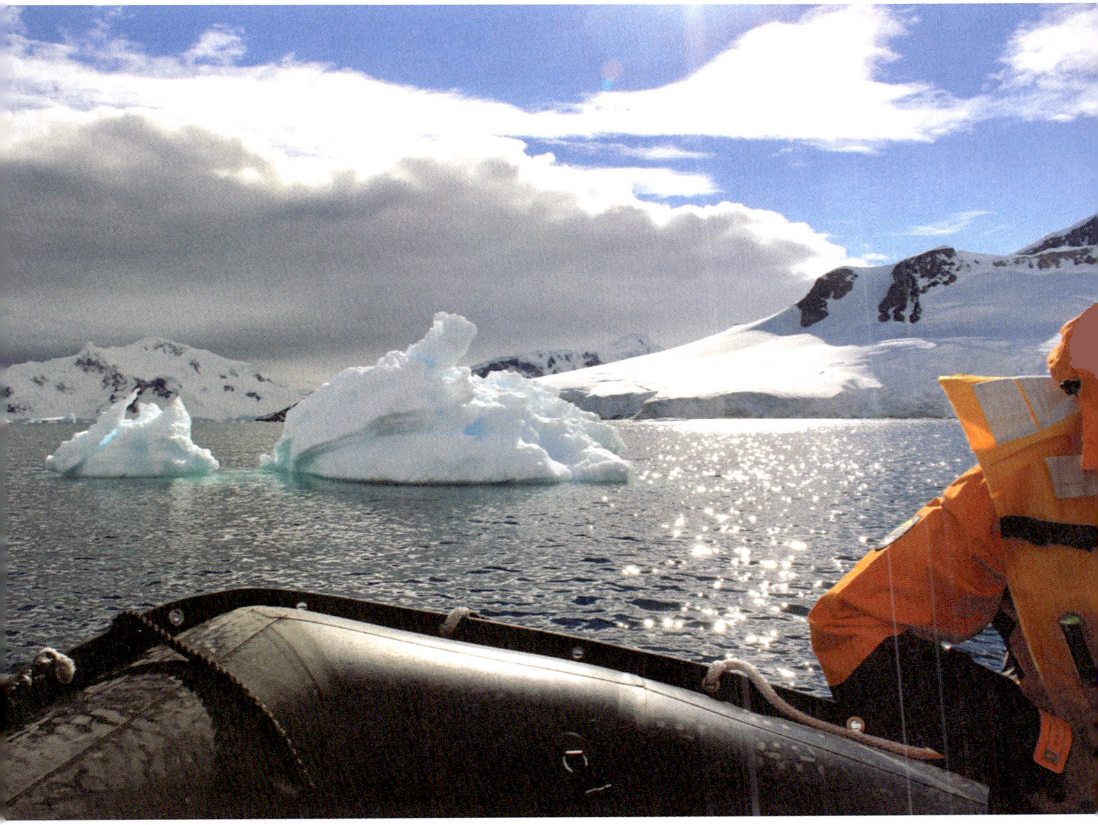

aware that expeditions do not always go as planned.

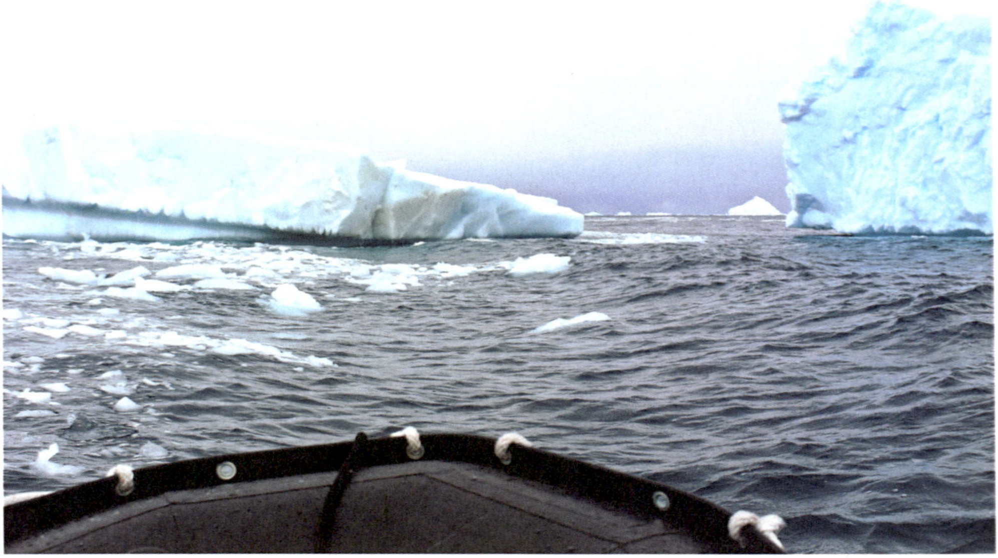

SAILING is especially tenuous with unforeseen weather changes through iceberg filled waters,revealing themselves at the last possible moment.

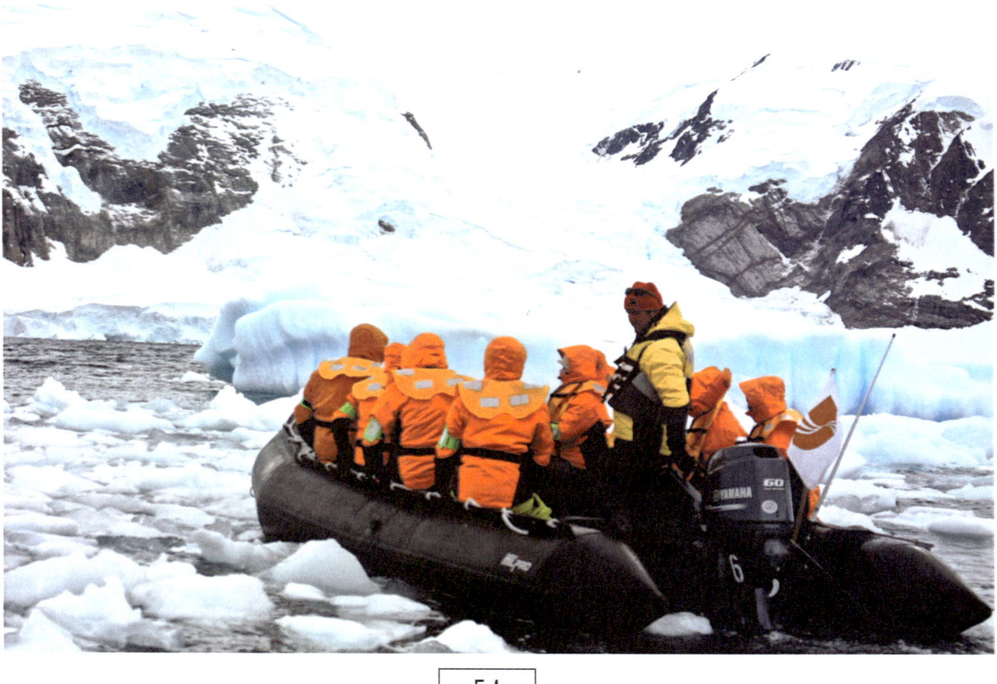

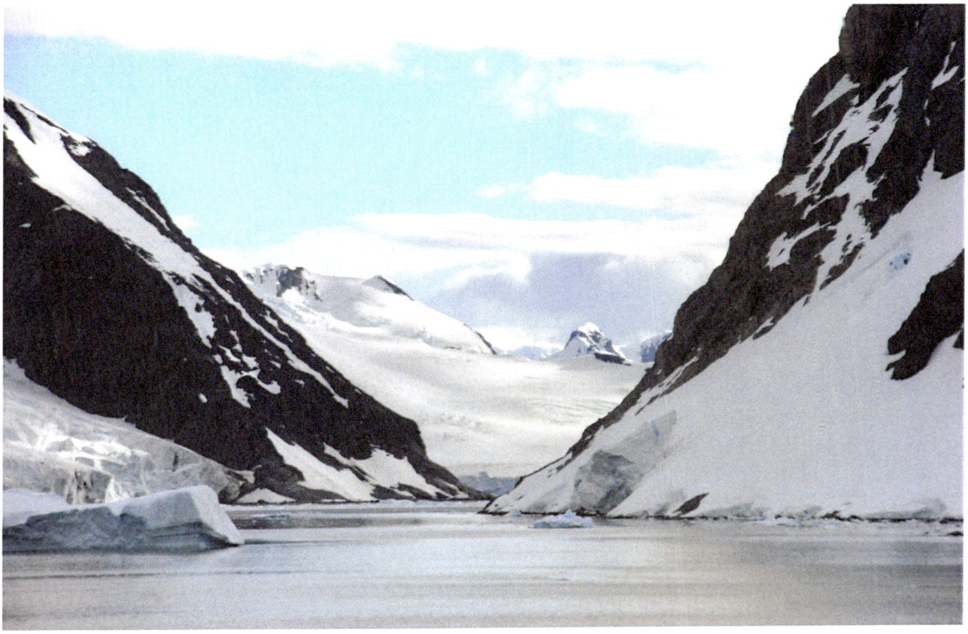

The rare opportunity to sail farther south than other ships had previously sailed ignites the adventurous spirit as each methodical movement of the ship stuns the eyes with spectacular views seen only by a few...

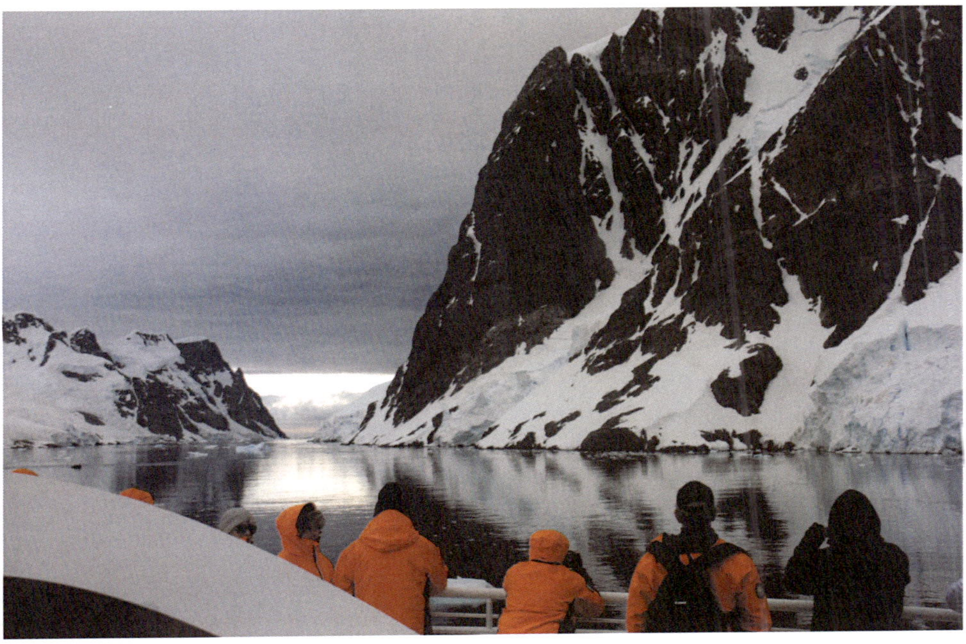

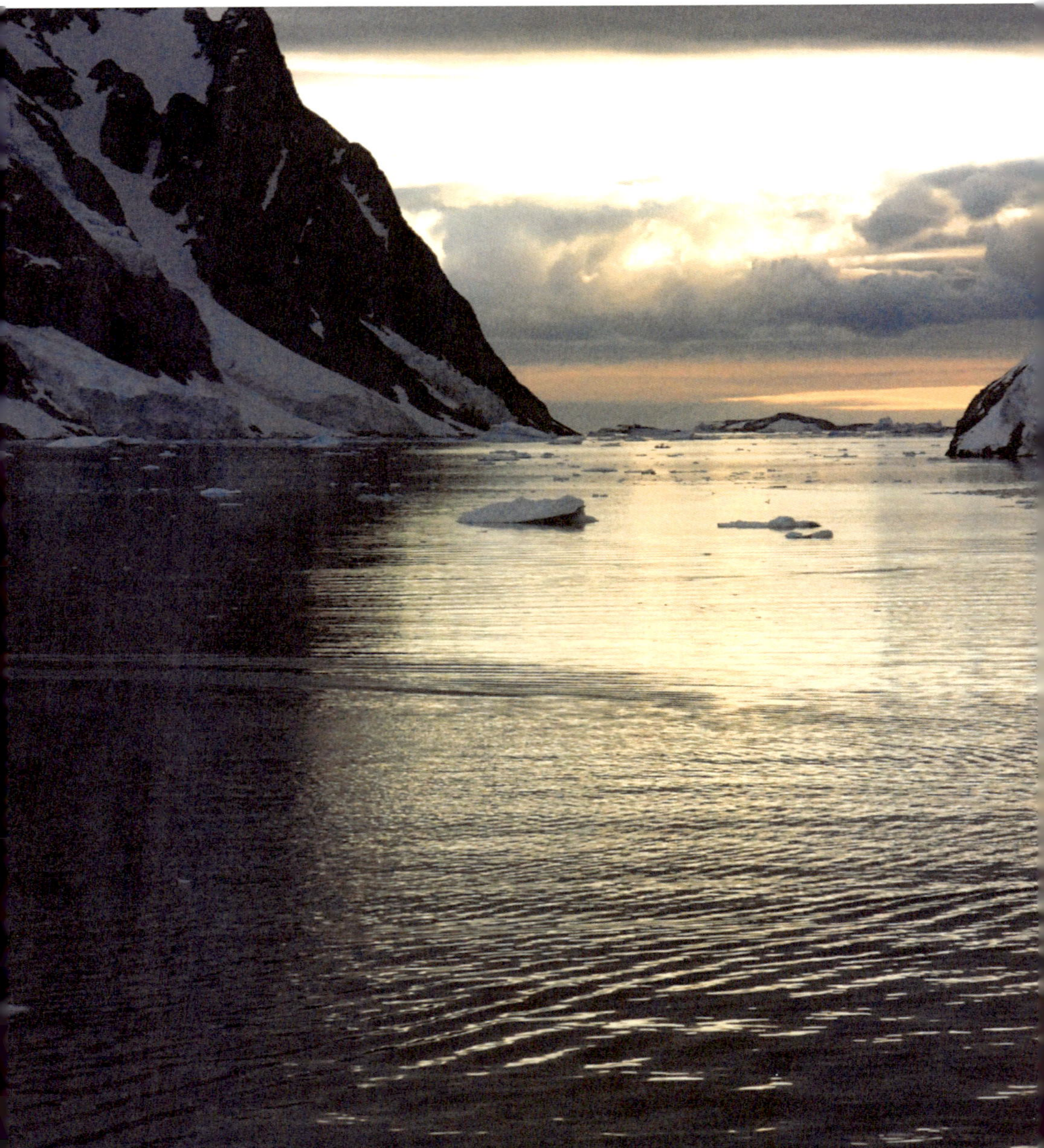

... as the captain chases the sunset through

LEMAIRE CHANNEL.

The vastness and minuteness, the complexity and simplicity, the beauty and potential hazard of the expedition to the seventh continent can only be assimilated by one's spirit.

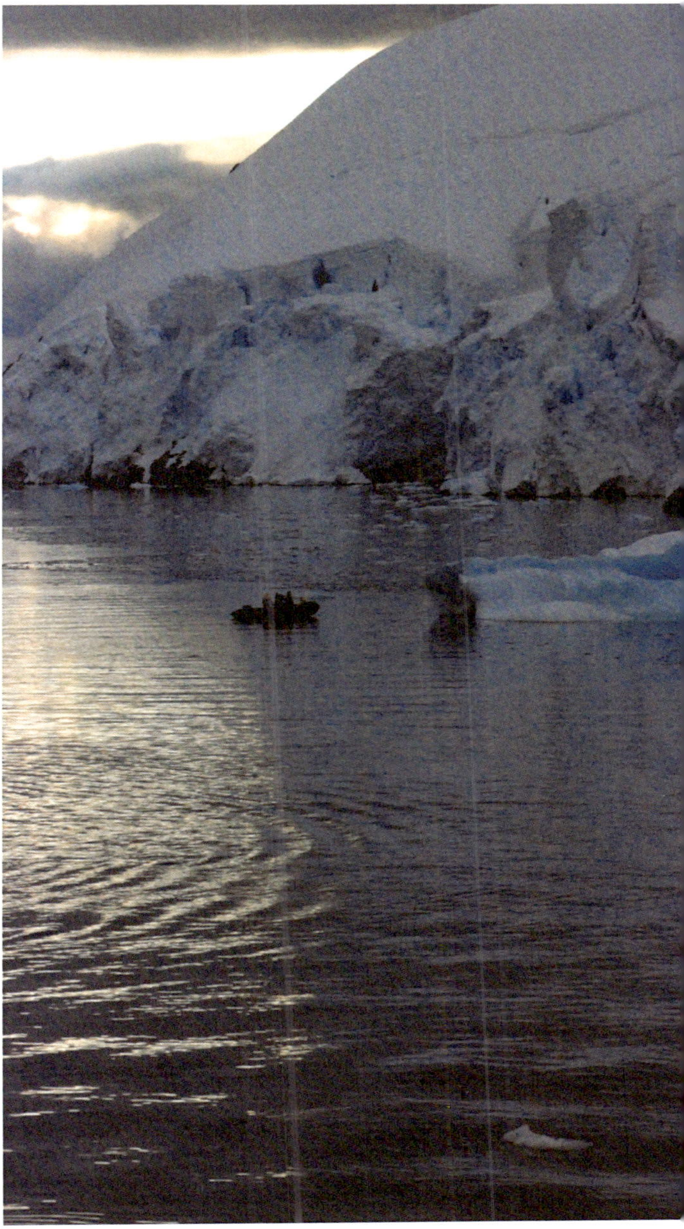

Even when the traveler tries to remember the magnificent glaciers, white with finely filigreed neon-blue tubes of ancient ice...or the unique ice carvings sparkling in the sunlight... or the hundreds of penguins, seals and whales sliding in and out of the ice filled water, unruffled and unafraid... or the exhilarating sense of unpolluted air filling one's lungs, he soon covets every photograph that attests to the fact that this adventure actually did occur in all of its spectacular beauty. Antarctica can only be experienced; it can never be adequately expressed.

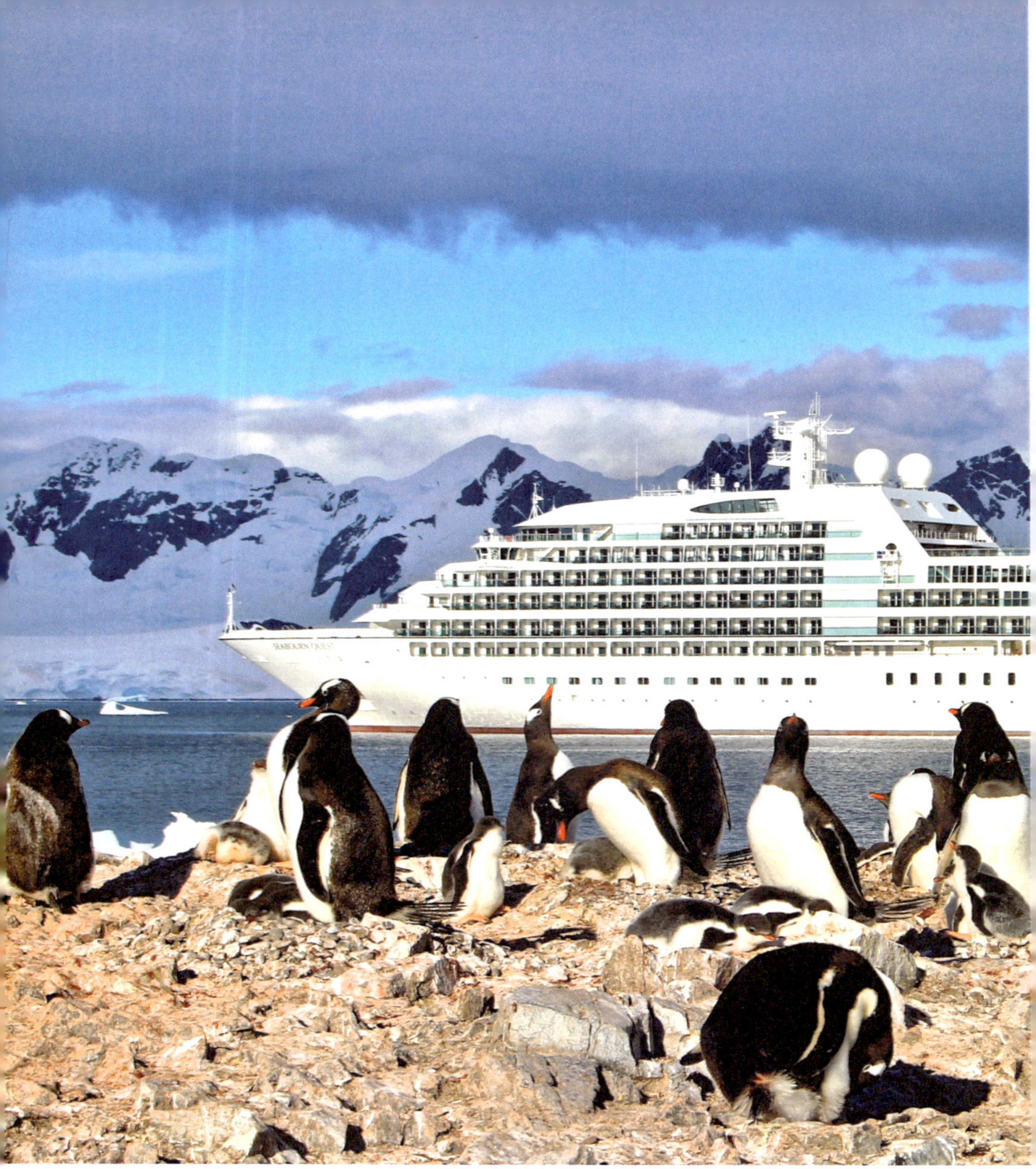

"In memories we were rich. We had pierced the veneer of outside things. We had suffered, starved and triumphed, groveled yet grasped at glory, grown bigger in the bigness of the whole.

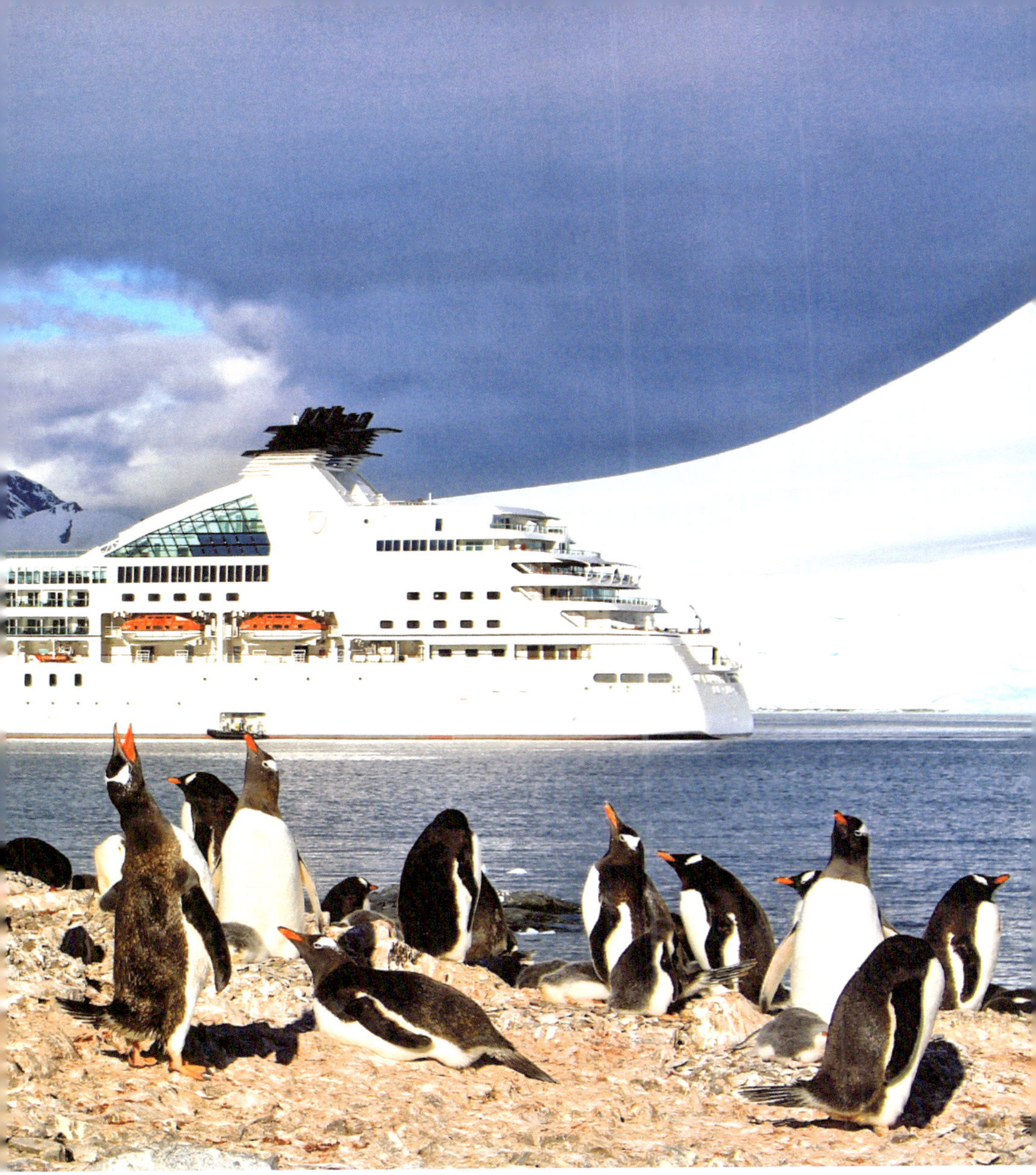

We had Seen God in his splendor, heard the text that nature renders. We had reached the naked soul of man..."

– SIR ERNEST SHACKETON

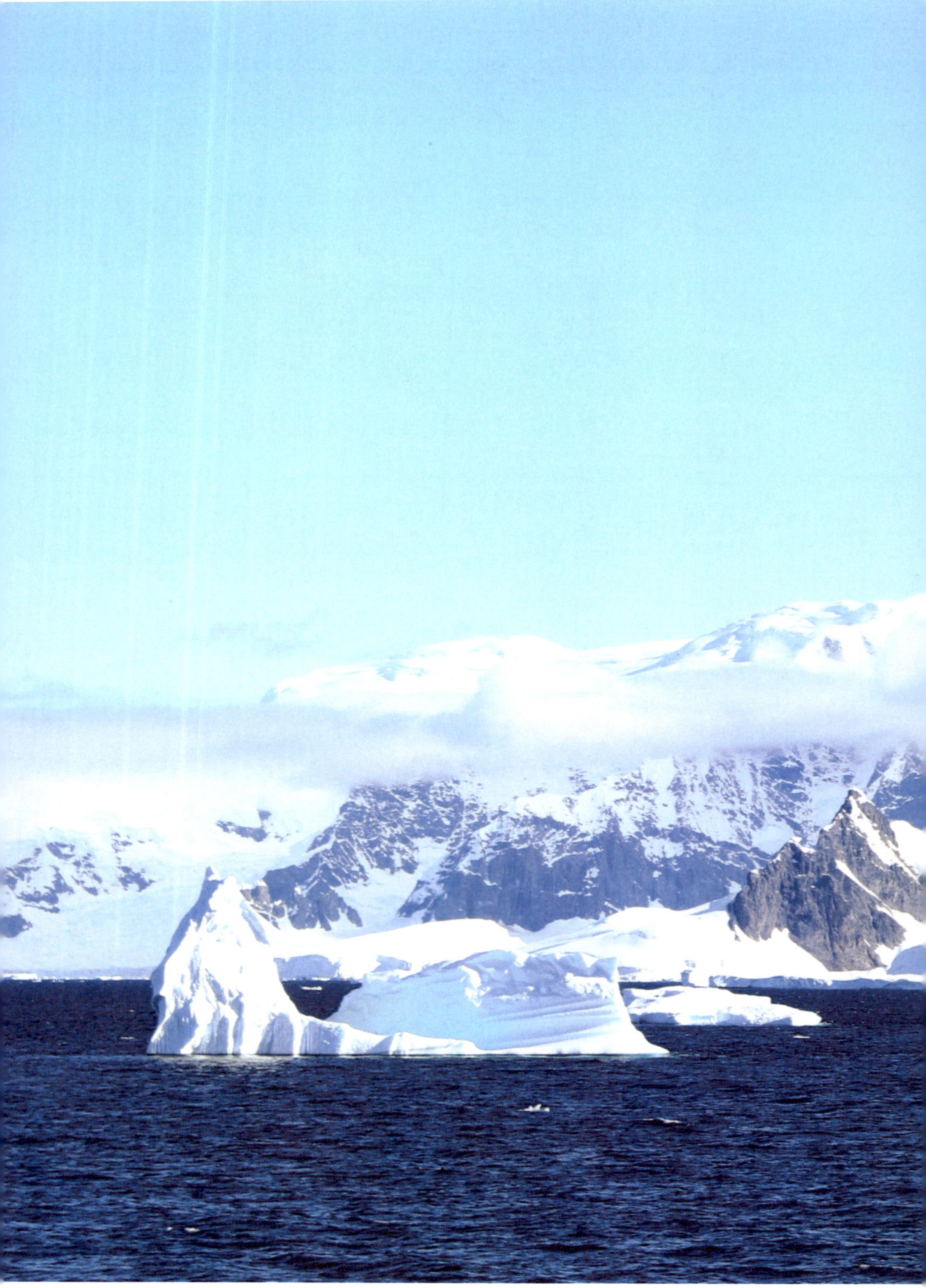

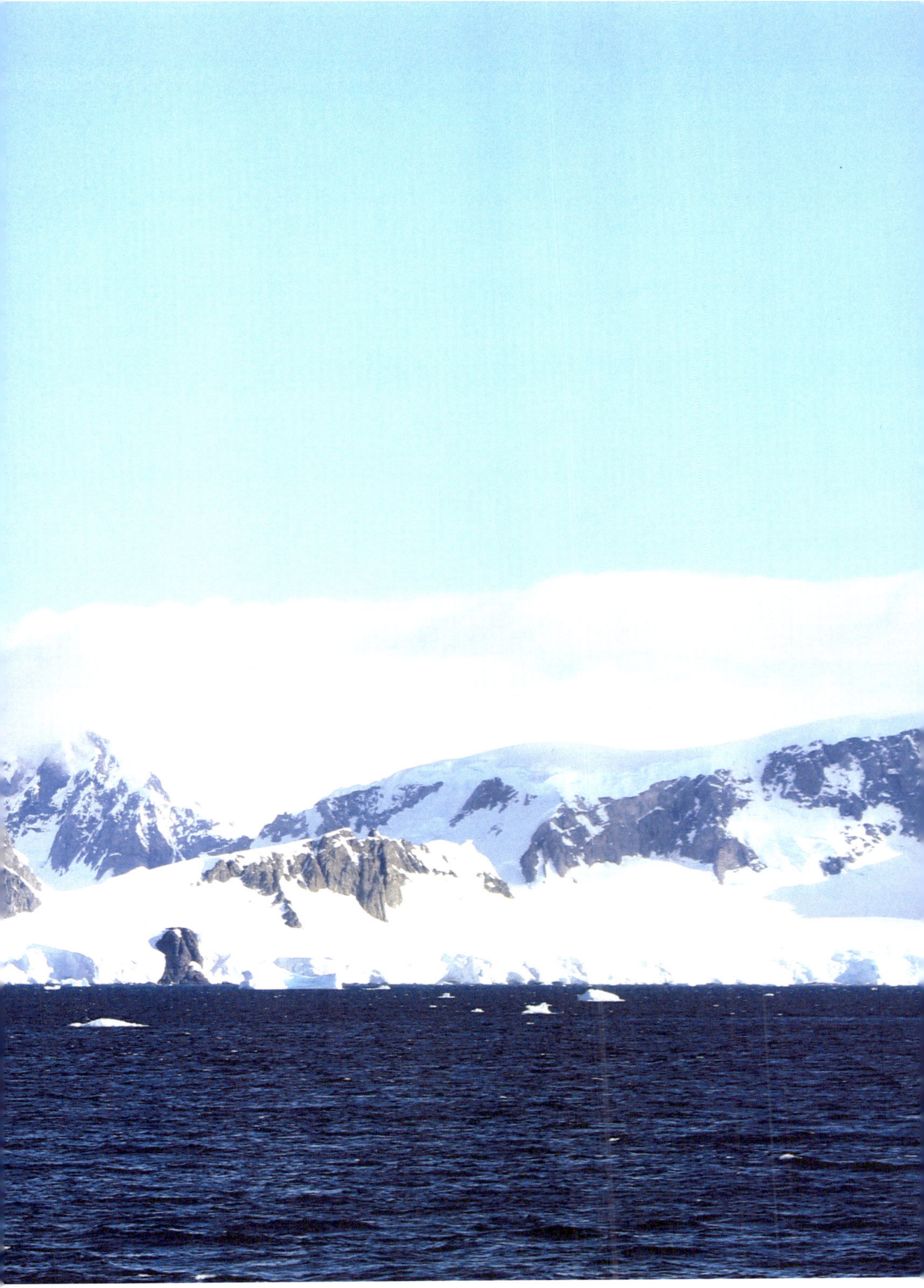

ABOUT *the* AUTHORS

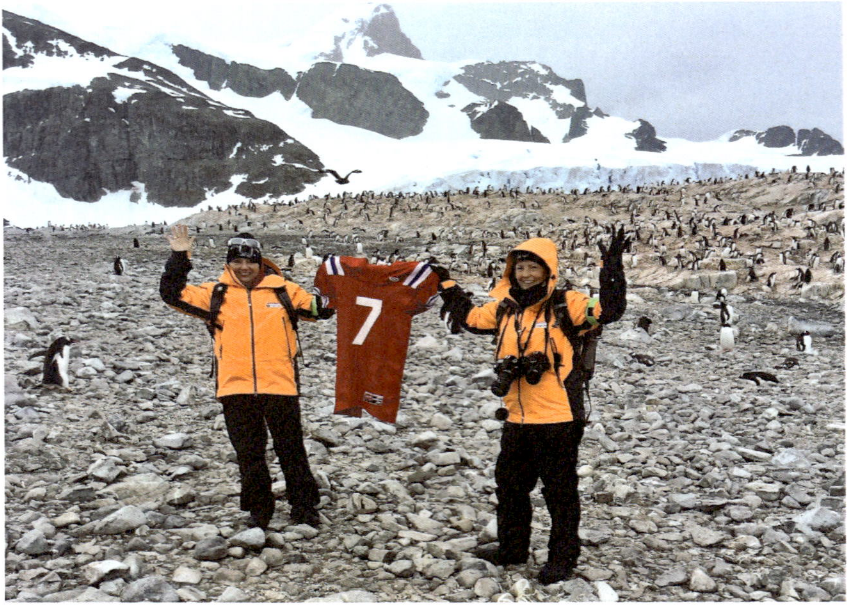

Pat Chapman and Martha Ellis, Louisiana natives who have spent most of their lives in the field of education as both teachers and counselors, have more recently broached their passion for knowledge and people using the world as their textbook, travelling to all seven continents. Current endeavors include authoring books using their travel photography to express the simple wonders of this world and its people.

CPSIA information can be obtained
at www.ICGtesting.com
Printed in the USA
LVRC101247021221
704874LV00019B/1

9781739810498